EXPLORING CELTIC SPIRITUALITY

Exploring
Celtic Spirituality

Historic Roots for Our Future

Ray Simpson

Hodder & Stoughton
LONDON SYDNEY AUCKLAND

British Library Cataloguing in Publication Data
A record for this book is available from the British Library

ISBN 0 340 64203 3

Typeset by Hewer Text Composition Services, Edinburgh
Printed and bound in Great Britain by
Cox & Wyman, Reading, Berks

Hodder and Stoughton Ltd
A Division of Hodder Headline PLC
338 Euston Road
London NW1 3BH

Contents

Acknowledgements

I dedicate this book to the Christian community of Bowthorpe, Norwich, whom I have served as founding minister for seventeen years, and who have offered me a pattern of worship and work, prayer and love that has enabled me to respond to the callings of God on my life.

In particular I owe an enormous debt to Frances, Helen, Maisie and Sue, who have given unstinting help with typing; and to my sister Sally, who has enabled 'space' to be kept in my life so that I could fully concentrate on writing this book.

I thank my friends Michael Mitton and Russ Parker for reading the first draft and for making useful suggestions, and Russ for writing the Preface. I am also grateful to Kate Tristram for allowing me to use the library at Marygate House, on the Holy Island of Lindisfarne.

The cover photo is by Cornelius Cullen

The drawing of Pilgrim's Way, Holy Island, is by David Colman

Preface

'It is the best of times, it is the worst of times.' This opening line from Charles Dickens' book, *A Tale of Two Cities*, describes very well the maelstrom of spiritual upheaval through which the Church is currently journeying. At the heart of some of this turbulence lies both a question and a quest. The question is whether the Church has become spiritually bankrupt and has outrun its usefulness. The quest is an older and deeper issue and has to do with the need for renewal, relevance and roots. There are those who have said that the Church has become powerless and have consequently looked elsewhere for their experience of signs and wonders; to some extent this has given rise to an amorphous collection of spiritualities commonly generalised under the heading of the New Age. Other critics reflect on the apparent inability of the established Church to adapt its ways and teachings to meet with the modern concerns of ecology, love of the earth and changing lifestyles with its resurgence of desire for true community.

The concern for roots gives expression to the age-old need to belong; to be cradled and connected by a faith which not only links a person with their history and culture but also provides a meeting place between the earth and heaven. This latter is surely why we are witnessing at the end of the twentieth century a growth in pilgrimage to holy places, be it Lourdes or the Vineyard church in Toronto, where God's power and presence have been located.

It should not surprise us therefore to find a growing interest in the life and witness and teaching of the Celtic Church because it weaves together all the strands of this quest. Here was a Church that was familiar with the powers of the Holy Spirit and which showed a friendly dynamic in its evangelism and witness to the pagan 'old agers' of its day. It was a Church without walls which wrapped itself in and around the community. The Celtic Church blended liturgy with imagination and hailed its poets and singers within a discipline of holiness and helps which endeared it to its people.

Ray Simpson has provided us with a feel and a glimpse of a spirituality which is now re-emerging from the mists of time to which an all too rigid Church had consigned it. His book helps us to get beyond nostalgia for all things old and enables us to appreciate their way of being. He then challenges us to learn the lessons and principles from that Church which was the first charismatic explosion of the faith in these islands and then find ways to apply them for our day. It is my belief and hope that Ray has given us a good resource to learn from our Celtic saints a way of being renewed in Christ, so that we too can continue our journey of faith for the love of God and others.

Russ Parker
March 1995

Celtic Christianity at a Glance

Long before conflicts so tragically divided Christianity, the Celtic Church came to flower. It existed from the fifth to the twelfth centuries. The Celtic churches were orthodox in faith but diverse in practice, evangelised and maintained unity through friendship, respected women's gifts, felt spiritually linked to creation, celebrated God through all the senses, inspired multitudes to holy lives of prayer, were bathed in the supernatural, and kept learning alive through the Dark Ages.

The mission sent from Rome in 597, which reflected the 'civil service' model of the Roman Empire, worked in harmony with the Celtic mission at times, but gradually the regulations of the Roman Church were enforced, the clergy became dignitaries, the Church grew less biblical, less charismatic, less close to the soil and to the poor. Much that was good and necessary was brought in, but comfort, pomp and uniformity assumed too large a place.

B.C.	The Celts, known as 'the fathers of Europe', emerged from Europe's heartlands as a distinct race, but under the Roman Empire retreated to western fringes such as Gaul, Britain and Ireland.
A.D.	After Christ
40/50	St Paul converts the Celts of Galatia.
43–410	Romans occupy southern Britain – Christianity is established with a few bishops.
313	Once the Emperor Constantine makes Christianity official, the Church slides into immorality and declines, but a counter-movement of Christians in deserts models holy lives.
390	Inspired by the desert Christians, Martin in Gaul and his apprentice, Ninian in Whithorn, Galloway, found mission communities of radiant Christians.
410	After the last Roman troops leave Britain, Anglo Saxon invaders destroy most remaining churches, except in the western fringes.
435	In Ireland, a century of evangelism begins by Patrick, Brigid,

Brendan, Columba, which leaves a 'land of saints' shaped by large communities of faith, with home-grown leaders.

450   In Wales, and Cornwall, a century of planting mission communities inspired by the desert Christians, by Germanus, Illtyd, Samson, Petroc, David, leave them lands of faith.

560   Columba spreads mission communities in Iona and Scotland.

591   Columbanus and others found mission communities throughout Europe.

597   The Bishop of Rome sends a mission team led by Augustine which eventually develops a national organisation and a spirituality that seems oppressive to the Celtic churches.

635   Aidan is sent from Iona to start a mission to the English from Lindisfarne. With its partner community at Whitby, led by Hilda, it sends missionaries to the East (Cedd) the Midlands (Chad) and further south.

664   The disastrous Synod of Whitby deals with the growing differences between Roman and Celtic ways by enforcing Roman regulations, e.g. about the date of Easter. Cuthbert and Hilda sadly accept these for the sake of unity, but maintain the Celtic spirituality. The Roman regulations are accepted in 696 in northern Ireland, 716 in Scotland, 755 in Wales.

690   The Golden Age of study and art. The *Lindisfarne Gospels* are inscribed, and later the *Book of Kells*.

793   A century of Viking invasions destroys monastic communities.

The Celtic fire continued in the hearts of Christians in the highlands, islands and western fringes in prayers, customs and holy places. Varying strands of Celtic spirituality are reflected in, for example, Welsh and Cornish eisteddfods, liturgies of the Scottish churches, Irish life and song.

1938   The Iona Community is founded by George McLeod and its abbey re-built.

1990s   As the Age of the Enlightenment ends, waves of re-kindled Celtic spirituality bring hope.

1994   The Community of Aidan and Hilda is founded.

Readers who wish simply to learn about features of Celtic spirituality should start to read at Part Two, Chapter 2.

Part One:

Roots for a Culture Change

1

The Call of Aidan Today

'Before you were born I selected you' (Jeremiah 1:5).[1]

I was conceived just before Hitler declared war on Great Britain. Hence my womb life was a series of trots, accompanied by sirens, into underground air-raid shelters. War played havoc with my early years, and my boyhood was often unhappy. Twice I ran away, and once I set fire to the local common.

Nature, though – the river, the flowers, the wild places – provided me with a solace. The world depicted in the Bible also attracted me, but I was too confused to let it become part of my everyday life. Eventually I did make a commitment to Christ, and started going to church. Though much was alien in the worship, one aspect touched me: the sense of history. Even the liturgy seemed to be a vehicle of continuity. I sensed that my new experience was not an isolated incident: it was part of a tapestry that God was weaving across the ages.

God had come into the 'front door' of my life, but the 'doors' of the other rooms were still firmly shut. When I reached the sixth-form at school, I went through a phase of cynical unbelief. Marxism gripped me. To me, Marxists had a passion, a philosophy, and a plan to redirect the course of history. Admittedly, the believers I read about in the Bible also had these qualities, but, to me, today's Christians seemed only to *talk* about religion; at best, it only affected their private lives.

In my case, even my private life was unhappy at this time. My parents planned to move away, and I failed an exam I needed in order to take up a place to read history at university. As to career, nothing was clear except my fantasies: farmer, Prime Minister, or boxing champion! I felt increasing desperation, so one Good Friday I spent three hours praying on my knees, 'God, if there is a God, show me what you want me to be, and I'll do whatever you want for the rest of my life!'

The following Monday, my friend and I got lost in thick fog as we cycled to a barn dance. Eventually we decided to ask the next person we saw to give us directions; this person happened to be an old lady. She told us the way, but then she started to ask us questions, and announced to me with a firm stare: 'Young man, the Lord is calling you to full-time ministry for him.' She told us that she had once had a missionary call, but had been medically unfit to take it up. She declared, 'That mantle God gave me I am now placing upon you.' Though I felt dazed by the import of what she was saying, the idea slowly percolated through to me that I had to do something in response to this encounter. I floated the idea of ordination to my local vicar, and then decided to explore ways of commencing theological training.

Over the next two years, while testing out my call to ordination, I experienced the dole queue, and jobs as school teacher, nursing assistant, coalman, stand-in restaurant manager, and shop-floor factory worker. Despite the variety, these jobs hardly prepared me for the shock of becoming the youngest theological student at the London College of Divinity, where I eventually completed the four-year London BD course.

During my time there, I learned much from the teachings on the prophets and church history, but I was too much of an introvert to enjoy the camaraderie at college, which to me seemed oblivious to the inner life of prayer, to the sacraments, or to community. A few people, though, exuded a gracious, prejudice-free attitude to my individuality, which made me feel good. Two of these men became archbishops: Janani Luwum was later assassinated by Idi Amin for being a true shepherd to his people, and of course George Carey went on to become Archbishop of Canterbury.

Learning to be a minister

I was ordained in 1964 in the Cathedral at Lichfield, a place that was first evangelised in the seventh century by Chad, one of the brothers of the Lindisfarne monastery. Chad's prophetic visions and powerful healings were a far cry from the grim routine of duty that characterised my first curacy in the Potteries. However, my rector did manage to teach me one essential precondition of a prophetic ministry: to get my conviction from God alone, and to take responsibility for carrying it through. This rector practised what he preached, and got up early each day to listen to God for direction about matters of the moment.

Waves of black immigrants were pouring into the area when I arrived in 1968 for my second curacy at Upper Tooting, south-west London. It was the time when Enoch Powell made his infamous 'rivers of blood speech', which undid in a day my two years' work of building up racial relationships. Although both my vicar, Jack Torrens, and I were firmly committed to a ministry to all races, many white people moved out of the area as black people poured in, and frictions steadily grew. Eventually, the stress made Jack ill. Thus we asked God to give us a strategy that would make sense of our ministry. In response to our prayers, we felt God was saying to us, 'Build the peace of the world in the streets of London'.

During this curacy, I was offered a room one morning a week at South West London College, where over half the students were from Africa. Students of different religious faiths would meet in the vicarage and have a time of silence – for Christians to listen to the Holy Spirit, for Muslims to listen to Allah, or for Hindus to listen to the inner voice. Everyone knew, though my vicar and I were committed to Christ, that they would not be pressed to convert against their will: there was a mutual trust. In fact, on one occasion a Hindu brought a Muslim to me and said: 'He wants you to tell him about Jesus Christ'. This taught us all a lesson about evangelism in a multi-faith society: that the best evangelism is done from a position of human fellowship with those who are not Christians. Undoubtedly, we had stumbled on one of the keys to the original evangelisation of these isles by the Celts.

Yet a huge block to evangelism at the time was the unwelcoming attitude of the white churches. These open-hearted newcomers from other countries were alienated by the very Church of England whose calling is to model hospitality. I witnessed faith and humanity die in innumerable black immigrants as they were faced with the cold attitudes in many of our churches. If only these native Anglicans had been in touch with their Celtic roots, they could have offered the newcomers the rhythm in worship, the warmth in fellowship and the awareness of God's presence in everyday life that they craved.

Hugh Montefiore, my suffragan bishop in the Southwark diocese, had started to discuss my becoming the incumbent of a parish, when out of the blue came an invitation to me to work for the Bible Society. The Society had a fresh vision to communicate the word of God, not only to the peoples of the world, but also to the cultural sub-groups in the United Kingdom. Hugh Montefiore felt that my personality would suit this challenge, and strongly advised me to accept the post.

This new post took me to East Anglia. Here, I related to some 1,323 churches and chapels, to schools, bookshops, prisons and local Action Groups. I travelled a great deal, loved the work, and made hundreds of friends and acquaintances. Yet there were still two huge gaps in my life, which sooner or later had to be filled.

The first gap was in my personal life. The fear that did not allow me to know myself, or be fully known by others, needed to be healed. While I was based at Thetford I became more aware of the work of the Holy Spirit; and thus began a process of real inner healing. The second gap was that between the Church I read about in the Acts of the Apostles and the churches I encountered in my travels. The Bible Society had allowed me to do some research on communicating the Bible to people in rural areas, and through this I learned that the Bishop of Ely believed that some parts of the Fens had *never* been converted. In a paper on this theme to the Evangelical Alliance, I concluded: 'The ground is so hard, and the people so pagan, that perhaps nothing less than a community of love in action will suffice to transplant the Body – the Life – of Christ. A community where some work, play, learn, sing in close inter-action with the native inhabitants, and which prays and shares freely together – why cannot evangelicals respond to such a challenge as do the followers of St Francis and others?'[2]

An experience that helped to bridge this gap came in the summer of 1978 while I was visiting relatives in Ireland. It was then that I found myself pouring out tears to God on a mountainside. 'Teach me to really love people', I cried. A very real spiritual encounter followed, and throughout the long journey home these words from God burned in my heart: 'Accept that you are a pastor'. The very week that I returned from Ireland, I received a letter from Maurice Wood, Bishop of Norwich, inviting me to become the first minister of a united Christian church in a community-in-the-making near Norwich.

Christian community

Bowthorpe comprises three linked urban 'villages', a blend of council and private houses, with a large shopping centre, and historic Bowthorpe, with a worship centre and workshops at its heart. The story of how Bowthorpe came into being has been told elsewhere.[3] All that needs to be said here is that as soon as I was shown round this community with one main centre next to a conservation area, something that seemed like a set of slides drifted into my mind. I knew with certainty that God wanted to plant a community of love at the heart of this new neighbourhood, and to create a healing environment in which wounded people could come to faith and wholeness.

Slowly, the community grew; and in spite of our frailties, God wrought his chemistry. As a local ecumenical project we were formally linked to six denominations; yet in the eyes of the residents, we were one family of Christians bound up in the neighbourhood's life. Words spoken through the prophets long ago seemed to apply to us: 'Your people will rebuild what has long been in ruins, building again on the old foundations' (Isaiah 58:12). I soon realised that these words applied more widely than to Bowthorpe alone.

Another part of the vision at Bowthorpe was that we would be open to each of the great streams within Christianity. Lesslie Newbigin had identified three major streams: the Catholic (incarnation and creation); Protestant (biblical proclamation and conversion); and Orthodox/Pentecostal (the mystical and the Spirit). We were not to be harnessed to only one, or even two, of these streams.

In stages, a Worship and Work area developed in the conservation area where the three villages and the main shopping centre converge. It consists of a new Worship Centre linked to the ruins of the ancient parish church, workshops for the handicapped in the renovated former harness sheds, a retreat cottage, a prayer cell in the old blacksmith's forge, and church community house, where I live. Also, local Christians are converting a large barn nearby into a sports and leisure centre for the area.

In 1985, as part of three months' sabbatical leave I visited the Holy Island of Lindisfarne, at the suggestion of a friend. I trod the earth where Aidan established the mission community that evangelised much of England in the seventh century. I felt that

Lindisfarne really spoke to me – perhaps because the spirit of the place has not been swamped by ecclesiastical or secular exploiters. After this first visit, I returned to the island every year.

At about this time my bishop, Peter Nott, asked me to explore whether I felt I had a calling to the religious life; I duly explored this with Benedictines, Carmelites, a Jungian-trained spiritual director, and with the Franciscans. I stayed at the Franciscan Retreat House at Glasshampton at the time that the Church of England was reeling from the infamous 'Crockford Preface' affair. (The anonymous author of the Preface to this directory of clergy had made scathing criticisms of the Church and committed suicide once his identity was found out.) All my energy was focused not on my personal search, but upon the soul of the national Church. Instead of producing a personal journal, as many do on retreat, I wrote an article entitled 'An Alternative Crockford Preface'. I had this printed as pamphlets and sold them; I also sent copies to fifteen bishops. One magazine printed an article containing the criticisms that formed the first part of the pamphlet, but omitted the eight targets for the Decade of Evangelism that formed the second part. The eighth target was a renewal of the Religious life of the Church of England, that is, of formal religious communities of monks, nuns or lay people, and of informal associations of people with vows. This revival would include publications of a daily worship book for 'non-bookish' people, revival of communities committed to mission, and a new lay order that linked people who are called to be signs of God's faithfulness in their own locality.

The renewal of Religious life

This section of the pamphlet began: 'The soul of the church is fuelled by its religious life. We are at a moment of *kairos*. With sufficient discernment and care, we can lay the foundations for a Religious life in the Church of England for the next hundred years, which will flower in a way we have not seen since the Reformation. This flowering must be English and evangelical as well as catholic, diverse as well as demanding.' I went on to describe a vision I had had: a large old oak tree in an apparently shapeless wood was uprooted in a gale. As planners surveyed the scene, wondering what to replace the oak with, someone noticed that two lines of self-seeded young trees were already shooting up; if they were recognised and given the right management, they would make a spacious avenue beside which the single old oak tree paled into lesser significance. The pamphlet continued in the following vein: even as some traditional Orders die, new forms of community rise up. As these become open to the listening and pilgrimage of their members, and as they dialogue with people in the world's crossroads, they will become instruments of God for our time.

With reference to the active encouragement of mission-based sketes (loose monasteries where each individual has their own dwelling and freedom to choose their work), linked to Christian shrines, monasteries, retreat centres or churches, I wrote:

> The sketes of the early desert Fathers, as our own Celtic hermitages, were an alternative to the completely ascetic solitary life and to the completely common life of the highly organised monasteries. They formed a base for mission. At a time when the whole church needs to recover its simplicity and humanity, the establishment of a variety of these is essential . . . Why should there not again be fifty people linked to one of these in a place such as Lindisfarne?

Brother Ramon the Guardian at Glasshampton felt, as did others whom I had consulted, that God was calling me, but not to an enclosed Order. This affirmed my belief in the value of 'the contemplative in the market place', and of what was growing at Bowthorpe. One of several bishops who responded to my Alternative Crockford Preface that I sent with a covering letter also wondered whether God might be calling me.

A new cradling

On 31 December 1987, while staying at Lindisfarne, I watched the Archbishop of Canterbury's New Year television message. I had decided to return to Lindisfarne in the depths of the winter solstice, when it was dark and damp, visitors were drunk, and the vicar of that time despaired of his empty church. This visit, I thought, would reveal whether my attraction to Lindisfarne was merely romantic, buttressed by the sunshine of summer visits.

The Archbishop of Canterbury's message was about the value of 'cradle places' – illustrated by Canterbury, which was preparing for the forthcoming Lambeth Conference. When the message was over and I had switched the television off, I went out alone into the black night, and fumbled my way into a little prayer cell that had been fashioned out of a stable – a stable, the cradle place for Christ – and there I knelt on the cold ground and offered up to God the island, the nation and the Church of England. Something like an enormous crankshaft seemed to turn inside me. It felt as if God was saying, 'Canterbury is certainly one cradle, but there is another cradle that is rooted deeper in the soil, deeper in the soul of the people, deeper in the supernatural, a cradle required by the *kairos* of our time. This cradle, which has been lost sight of, is to be rediscovered; from it there will be a birthing of a New Way in the Church, which has a significance far beyond anything that one person can comprehend.' I knew with certainty that these words were from God. I returned to Bowthorpe and asked God to give me further guidance and direction.

In the spirit of Jeremiah (who purchased a field in faith that it would be needed when God revived Jerusalem), I bought, with the help of God and my sister Sally, Starbank Cottage, on the Holy Island of Lindisfarne, in February 1992, without even knowing how God meant me to use it. That same month, a leader of the Northumbria Community (a network of Christians in Northumbria) put out a prayer request: that accommodation on the island would be offered by Easter so that he could base his ministry there. Thus it was that Andy was ensconced in Starbank Cottage before Easter, and God worked wonders in the amazing influx of people who sometimes overflowed the house. Thus the cottage became committed to Holy Island life – it was not just another holiday home.

I had shared the vision of this 'cradling' of a new 'Way' in the Church with Michael Mitton, Director of Anglican Renewal Ministries, who asked me to write an article for the ARM magazine, *Anglicans for Renewal*. He took the manuscript to a conference at Durham where it disappeared, and – unusually – I had not kept a copy. So I sent Michael a recording of the article from memory, and much background material; he spent forty-eight hours immersed in this. The article spoke to him about a new direction for renewal. To Michael's surprise, God was speaking along similar lines to his wife, Julia, and to other colleagues. One such man was John Peet, who had retired early from a senior position in industry to convert large old buildings into a Christian Centre at Redhill, near Stratford-upon-Avon, through the Redhill Trust. He and his wife Jacquie felt called to live a Celtic spirituality, such as the following chapters define.

Michael Mitton and John Peet then made a retreat on Holy Island; and as they traversed its shores, a stream of prophetic words came to them which they scribbled down. Could these be seeds of a new way of life for the Church? Over the next two years, the seven of us met quarterly to pray, to grow in our relationships, to clarify and develop this new Way, and the specific details of living it. We consulted with various church leaders and others. The outcome was that we decided to establish what is now called the Community of Aidan and Hilda.

Aidan, a man of great gentleness, holiness and love, was the monk who came to Lindisfarne from Iona in 635, after the first mission of the Celtic Church to the English had failed. He has been called 'the apostle of the English'. Hilda, Aidan's great friend, was a Saxon who founded a monastery for men and women at Whitby, according to Aidan's principles, from which a stream of leaders evangelised much of England. Hilda was widely revered as 'Mother', and was described by the ancient historian Bede as a jewel that 'emitted such a brilliant light that all Britain was lit by its splendour'.

The Community of Aidan and Hilda is a scattered community, a body of Christians who share the belief that God is once again calling us to the quality of life and commitment that was revealed in the lives of the Celtic saints, who once so effectively evangelised the isles of Britain, Ireland and beyond. Its aim is 'the healing of the land through men, women and children who draw inspiration from the Celtic saints'. By the healing of the land, we mean both the people and the soil.

The Community has three objectives:

1 *To restore* – the memory, landmarks, witness and experience of the Celtic Church in ways that relate to God's purposes today.
2 *To research* – the history, beliefs, lifestyle, evangelism and relationships to cultural patterns of the Celtic Church; and how they apply to the renewal of today's Church and society.
3 *To resource* – through production of patterns of worship suitable for corporate, household and personal use; provision of retreats, seminars and conferences; and, above all, through a network of people.

We see the Community as being a series of circles. In the centre is God. The first circle consists of Members and Explorers who

adopt the Community's way of life. Each of these has a Soul
Friend (*anamchara*), who works with them to develop their own
way of life that is personally suited to them. It relates to ten
areas of life, which are explained in the common Way of Life of
the Community. These are: (1) study; (2) spiritual direction; (3)
daily prayer and work; (4) intercession; (5) lifestyle; (6) care for
creation; (7) wholeness; (8) openness to God's Spirit; (9) unity and
community; (10) mission. These areas are examined in more detail
in the Appendix on p. 195. Some people will want to continue in this
open-ended way without any pressure to be more than Explorers.
Others, who have completed at least a year and who sense this is
the road they are called to travel, may make trial vows. Vows with
a lifelong intention may later be made, though they continue to be
renewed year by year.

The second circle consists of Friends, who subscribe to our
Newsletter, pray, attend events we arrange in different venues,
or use our resources. A third circle consists of link churches
and centres who wish to explore a Celtic model of mission with us.
In the future we trust some will hear a call to live together in a
residential community committed to prayer, training and mission,
and to make life vows. We hope the first such community house
will be at Lindisfarne. The circles are 'held together' and served by
the Caim Council (Caim being the Celtic 'circling' prayer).

The Way was made public at a national Symposium at Swanwick
entitled 'Roots for Renewal' in March 1994. A delegate at the
Symposium had awoken one morning to a strong sound of rustling
trees, but they were not the trees at Swanwick. This reminded her
of an experience of King David at a time of threatened defeat.
He, too, heard the sound of the wind rustling in the trees. As a
result, he was given a new angle, a new way of approaching the
enemy, and this led on to victory and the turning of the tide (1
Chronicles 14:15). This image spoke to me. Was God calling us
to approach the enormous needs of the world in a new way? We
are not called to copy the old ways; we are called to be wholly
present to God so that the resurrections we receive from him are
deeply rooted. Was he providing us with a new angle through the
Community's Way?

We issued a response sheet at the Symposium. All sorts of
people showed interest, and the Reverend Jack Stapleton flew
3,000 miles from the States to be at the Symposium. Within a
few months, a US chapter of the Community had started, with

Jack as its chaplain. Individuals from four continents have now linked up with us. In Britain we formed the Caim Council, with Simon Barrington-Ward, Bishop of Coventry, as President.

The Redhill centre supplied an office, a Newsletter was launched, resource sheets were produced, and people were invited to join us. I was appointed as honorary Guardian of the Community, with prayer that financial provision would come to enable me to be employed full-time. Seven adults, with other family members, went by boat from Lindisfarne to Farne Island, where Cuthbert spent the last years of his life in prayer. We sat on the ground among the darting nesting birds, and made our vows.

We invited the poets Carol and Stewart Henderson to join the Caim Council as its bards. Bards played a key role in Celtic life. They were the storytellers, poets and songsters who, together with the seers who interpreted the meaning, passed on the message so that it touched parts the formal church functionaries could never reach. This enabled Christianity to survive fierce ideological onslaughts. We believe that today we are called to re-create a Christian imagination. In helping us to do this, we want to give our bards the place of honour they deserve.

In the period after the Symposium, a stream of inspiration was given that enabled the Community to produce experimental patterns of worship to meet a rising tide of needs. There is the need for 'street-wise' rituals that connect with people's hopes, fears and sorrows; the need to embrace the feminine equally with the masculine, the material along with the spiritual; the need to bridge the gap between formal church liturgies and creationist practices that are inspired by nature; the need to rediscover Christian roots that go back beyond the bureaucratic model established by Augustine that has shaped the Church in the West, to our endogenous Christian Celtic beginnings, which also draw on Jewish and Orthodox roots; the need to foster spontaneity within a framework that lights up our heritage; the need for worship that reflects the rhythm of creation and the flow of human life. Acts of worship in celebration of Celtic saints days are rolling off our computers; and patterns of worship for Christians who desire to pray daily in neither an individualistic nor a 'churchy' way.

We are in the Decade of Evangelism – the population is no longer familiar with Christian words and concepts; yet even occasional services of churches often assume the congregation is Christian, and thus devalue the services and the people who attend. There is a need for 'user-friendly' services that provide a vehicle for the good aspirations of participants, which lead them on to a next step in faith, but which do not assume they are committed Christians.

There are now about sixty members of the Community, and many more Friends. Retreats and special days have been held in different parts of the country, and my cottage at Lindisfarne is much used by members who wish to make individual retreats. A house in the Midlands has been offered to the Community as a small centre for healing and study, and we pray that a house may also be provided to give a focus for the Community at Lindisfarne. I have been asked to work full-time for the Community, and to work with link churches which seek to develop a Celtic model of mission. All this adds up to a large agenda that will take many years to deliver, but we are privileged to be able to play a part in it.

2

Culture Change

A decade ago, Alvin Toffler's book, *Future Shock*, seemed once removed from our lives. Yet now it is with us. We are in the midst of a massive cultural change that involves political, ecological, social and religious patterns. This is even recognised at the most basic level of rock music. The singer Neil Young likens our culture to an empty supermarket trolley. In response, his music taps into the yearning for a naked sincerity, new frontiers and wide open spaces.

When I first shared my call to cradle a spirituality in the spirit of St Aidan, I wondered if it would resonate with anyone else. I need not have worried. This spirituality resonates with those who are addressing cultural changes from widely differing perspectives. In the following pages, the term 'Celtic spirituality' refers to the Christianity of people such as Aidan and Hilda. They championed the Christian faith, yet were free from Roman stereotypes of Christianity, and were open enough to respond to fresh adventures of God's Spirit and to the concerns of an evolving people.

Celtic spirituality resonates with thinkers who are addressing the sea change in our western culture. A growing number of thinkers are exposing the inadequacies of the Enlightenment mentality, and are predicting its end. The Enlightenment mentality prides itself that reason and science are the measure of all things. Not everything in the Enlightenment was bad, but its values have sown the seeds of their own destruction. Everything has been reduced to a commodity. Graham Cray, Principal of Ridley Hall, Cambridge, asserts that the culture of the western world from which the primary traditions of the Church of England take their form is approaching its demise. A whole world-view is collapsing. Our memory of our past and our sense of rootedness have been lost. Cray argues that this has brought about alienation, which destroys the unity of the human being as a creator of culture;

individualism, which destroys community; the divorce of rights from responsibilities; and the abuse of the created world.[1]

. The movement called 'The Gospel and our Culture', spearheaded by people such as Lesslie Newbigin, Alan Torrance and Andrew Walker, exposes the absurdity of the view that only things you can measure (such as food, gadgets or cars) are 'real', whereas things you cannot measure (such as God, love or beauty) are 'merely' subjective matters of taste. They demonstrate that factual knowledge is not separate from faith; in fact, it derives from it.[2] In his book *Real Presences*, George Steiner demonstrates that in the arts it is in fact 'the absence of God' that has led to disintegration, and where God's presence is no longer felt, 'certain dimensions of thought and creativity are no longer attainable'. Furthermore, in the realm of psychology, Carl Jung discerned earlier this century that western humanity, in dismissing what is 'primitive', had lost touch with aspects of reality that are primal and universal. It is this flight from reality that has led to neurosis and dis-ease in the soul of the people.[3]

Today there is a turning from secularism towards spirituality, but it is to any and every type of spirituality – except that of the churches, which are often identified with a bureaucratic, outdated culture. The emerging culture is the 'pick 'n' mix' variety, and the New Age movement, which seeks to embrace the energies within the universe, is the first attempt at a postmodern world-view. The challenge to Christianity is to find the appropriate way of communicating the gospel to a new culture as it forms; and to respond to the longing for a return to a holistic approach to life that does not put the natural and the supernatural, the sacred and the secular, into separate compartments. Many people see this holistic approach lived most gloriously in the Celtic Church in the sixth to tenth centuries, and wish to draw from this part of our heritage in order that a new culture may grow that will better serve the next century, and that a new Church that has a rootedness may grow up within and alongside the old Church.

Celtic spirituality resonates with political thinkers who recognise, after the fall of communism, the defects of capitalism, and look for another way. There is a swing towards nationalism today, but this is driven by fear – not by a renewal of trust. One American study states that 3,500 groups around the world describe themselves as 'nations', yet recognised nations only add up to about 180. Jaques Attali, former president of the European Bank for Reconstruction and Development, believes that a clear potential exists for up to twenty Yugoslav-type civil wars in Europe and the former Soviet Union alone. 'Xenophobia looks like becoming the mass ideology,' says the social commentator Eric Hobsbawm, 'what holds humanity together today is a denial of what the human race has in common.' The need to harness ethnic roots to a pure love of God and an outgoing love of humanity has never been so great; and it is the Irish, Scottish and Welsh of the sixth to tenth centuries who can teach us how to do this.

Celtic spirituality resonates with people who are concerned with evangelism. Evangelism, though, in the United Kingdom at least, has gained a bad name. The majority of church-goers dislike the term and cringe at the idea, for evangelism has come to mean 'strangers pressurising people by artificial means to accept something that is alien to them'. While churches are growing in many countries, their remorseless decline in Europe continues. Thinking people do not question the need for evangelism, but they know that more of the same sort of evangelism will fail to address the situation. Thus they are looking for radical new models, and a Celtic model is being put forward with increasing frequency.

The Church of England's Board of Mission stated in its *1993 Decade News*:

> The last time when this land was fundamentally non-Christian was 1,400 years ago when the Anglo-Saxon pagans conquered the land. How did our forefathers cope? Can we learn from their experience of evangelising a non-Christian culture? Evangelism sprouting from places of prayer and scholarship . . . evangelism which fits the society it addresses . . . evangelism reliant upon teams of Spirit-guided men and women . . .

Celtic spirituality resonates with those charismatics who see no future in a renewal culture that colludes with the consumer mentality, but does not renew our roots. Michael Mitton, Director of Anglican Renewal Ministries, has urged charismatic Anglicans in Singapore not to copy unthinkingly the culture of renewed Christians in Britain, but to let the Holy Spirit renew their own distinctive roots. On his return to Britain, Michael Mitton realised that charismatics in Britain were just as guilty of copying the imported 'flavour of the month' spirituality. Charismatic renewal has no future unless it touches what is truest and deepest in our British character.

Celtic spirituality resonates with Protestants who realise that the Reformation was not the last word on the things of God. The Reformation has been described like this: 'In biblical times God provided wells of salvation. During the centuries following, these wells became filled with junk. The Reformation cleared out the junk so we could get back to the original Christianity.' However, this description overlooks several facts. First, that despite corrupt and erroneous developments, there were also developments architected by God's Spirit. Second, it omits the fact that a significant number of 'wells' were overlooked by the Reformers: the 'well' of community and of relationships for example. Luther, the trail-blazer of the Reformation, whose temper was infamous, and whose bilious sermon about Jews was distributed by Hitler, had a blind spot here. Other 'wells' that were overlooked were the well of creation; the well of the praise of God through all that we have – the five senses and colour; the well of common morality.

Celtic spirituality resonates with people concerned with the future of the Church of England. Some have come to share the suspicion of G. K. Chesterton, the Roman Catholic writer, that modernism has taken endemic and debilitating root in the Church of England, which was defined by the liberalism of the Enlightenment, and lacks the true marks of Christ's Church. One of my most able Anglican theological friends told me that fifty of his Anglican colleagues had left to join the Roman Catholic Church or the House Churches because of this. Others were crossing over to the Orthodox Church.

Of course, the evangelical and catholic wings of the Church of England never placed themselves primarily in the liberal camp, but now the Book of Common Prayer and the inherited (male) priesthood were no longer binding on all, they began to polarise. Defensive groups such as 'Reform' and 'Forward in Faith' tended to define themselves by what they were against, and some wondered whether the Church was bound together only by the manners and money of the Establishment, both of which were diminishing fast.

The Celtic resurgence presented these people with a truer, more comprehensive, picture of the Church of England. It can usefully be pictured as a tree: some branches needed pruning, such as the branch that grew out of the Enlightenment. A large fork represents the Protestant/Catholic divide. Yet the trunk itself is large and strong, and the roots spread deep in the soil. These represent the original Church of the land, holy and biblical, catholic and indigenous, charismatic and orthodox – and a vehicle for all the senses.

Glyn, a practising Anglican, stayed with us for six months to sort out a mid-life crisis. 'I don't fit in the standard church,' he told me. 'What bits of you don't fit?' I asked him. 'I have a passionate and changeable temperament. I need to express these passions with my imagination, my body, with music and poetry. I feel as if the Church is designed for insurance clerks who never do anything with passion. I have a strong sense of place. I can sense holy ground, and when I do, I need to express it. I want a church that has local saints – I don't want either an absence of them, or centralised saints who live far away.'

Celtic spirituality resonates with Anglicans outside England too. One Canadian theologian told me that the Anglican Church in Canada, which now had neither the Book of Common Prayer nor the legal framework of Establishment, was adrift; many people were looking for an anchor. A US Episcopalian leader felt that the issue of homosexuality could be the final straw that would split his Church in two; and that many church people would be desolate wanderers looking for a birthright they were not even sure existed. If the picture these people had of the Anglican Church was true, their despair was justified. Moreover, their picture was distorted: they had seen what was on the surface, but had overlooked what lay underneath. They had missed the anchor and overlooked the birthright.

Celtic spirituality resonates with leaders of House Churches and other denominations. One House Church leader happened to hear some worship led by musicians of the Northumbria Community at a gathering for northern church leaders at Bradford Cathedral. Although he had no place for liturgy in his tradition, this Celtic-style worship reduced him to tears. He determined to find out what it was that had touched him so deeply, and so drove over 300 miles to meet members of the Northumbria Community who had been invited to my cottage at Lindisfarne. This man was always active, totally committed, a church planter. He read aloud some words pinned on to a book-end about there being a contemplative in all of us, and he began to weep; a new dimension of God was overwhelming him. He asked what it meant. Someone suggested that he represented one of many fresh streams of spiritual life flowing in the nation; these streams were recent and on the surface. Yet unknown to many, a much older stream had always been flowing underground, deep and pure. Now it was coming nearer the surface and these other streams were to cross it and even to flow together for part of their way.

A Roman Catholic from the Irish Republic attended the Swanwick Symposium. He felt that the patterns of worship we used were just what was needed in Ireland. The liturgies imposed in recent centuries had quashed the naturalness of people's spirituality, and of their relationship with their own saints. Ireland, too, is ready for a rediscovery of its roots.

We now go on to look in detail at this 'new/old' form of Christianity. It is a passionate love affair with God whose presence vibrates through all creation. It is creation-friendly and people-friendly, yet it engages in 'spiritual warfare'. It champions the orthodox Christian faith, yet it is flexible and diverse in its practices. It is free from bureaucracy and workaholism, yet is not sectarian. Like the patterns on the Celtic Bible manuscripts, these different strands are woven into a single whole.

3

Lindisfarne Landmarks

'Stand at the crossroads and look. Ask for the ancient paths, and where the best road is. Walk on it, and you will live in peace . . . My people have forgotten me . . . They have stumbled in the way they should go, they no longer follow the old ways . . . Set up signs and mark the road; find again the way by which you left. Come back . . .' (Jeremiah 6:16; 18:15; 31:21).

There is a longing for a new way of living that is true to our roots; and this call to rediscover God-given roots is part of a Bible-based faith.

In order to rediscover the 'old' way, we need to trace the ways of God's people in periods when they had not forgotten him. First, we must study those periods that are recorded in the Bible; second, we must learn how Christians first patterned his ways in our own lands. If we fail to do this, we will be unable to 'make sure' of God's way today. We have to learn the lessons God wants us to learn from these pioneers.

To 'set up guideposts' means we have to restore moral and spiritual ways, and I was reminded of this at Lindisfarne. Pilgrims who walk many miles to reach the Holy Island of Lindisfarne are confronted by treacherous tidal sands before they can reach their final destination. Fortunately, posts have been placed along the safe route, known as Pilgrims Way. Over the years, these posts became defaced or submerged, but in 1987 they were restored.

These posts at Lindisfarne can serve as a symbol of landmarks that have been almost lost sight of, but that now God calls us to restore. These landmarks go back beyond the Enlightenment, which was responsible for installing the false landmark of reason; and they go back beyond the Reformation – which although it

•

destroyed some false landmarks, also overlooked true ones. As we trace our Celtic Christian origins, the roads lead back to Wales, Cornwall and Ireland, to Iona where Columba arrived in the sixth century, and to Lindisfarne, from where Aidan and his teams evangelised much of England.

Each chapter in Part Two of this book explores one of these landmarks. These landmarks may be used as benchmarks of the spirituality that churches and groups could adopt. This approach has nothing to do with archaism, or copying for copying's sake; it is to do with finding inspiration and direction from God's hand in our history, in order to move on to a transfiguration of our future.

The late Martin Reith, who was a hermit priest, said at a gathering at Iona in 1991: 'The body of Christ is God's healing agency in the world. In Britain that Body needs healing itself. As we turn our attention to our forefathers in the Faith, we shall be jolted out of centuries of compromise and brought face to face with the Gospel in all its naked glory.'

> 'How wonderful it is to walk with God
> Along the road which holy men have trod'
> (Theodore H. Kitching).

> 'We will not have a sense of future until we
> regain a sense of rootedness' (Graham Cray).

Guideposts of the Lindisfarne Pilgrim Way

Part Two:

Lindisfarne Landmarks

John and the Eastern Connection

'In the beginning was the Word . . . through him God made all things . . . the Word became a human being' (John 1:1; 3:14).

The Celtic Church drew much inspiration from John, the beloved apostle of Christ, and from the first centuries of the churches of the east. The only New Testament letters penned in the name of Christ are those the risen Son of God gave to John, when he was in exile on Patmos. The relationship between John and Jesus was the most intimate and free-flowing of Jesus' relationships with the apostles. The Celtic Church, while it accepted the authority of Peter and of all the other apostles, had a special rapport with John, whom it looked upon as its spiritual father.

John spent the last part of his long life among the churches of Asia Minor (modern Greece and Turkey), and was thought of as the apostle of the eastern churches. At the Council of Whitby in the year 664, when Celtic and Roman spokespersons had to put their respective cases in order to decide whether Roman regulations (about such matters as the date of Easter and the form of baptism) had to be enforced upon the Celtic churches, Colman, for the Celts, rested his case on the fact that their customs over Easter were, as they presumed, handed down from John.

After Cuthbert, who was made Abbot of Lindisfarne after the Council of Whitby, had been healed of the plague, his great friend Boisil, who told him that he himself would die of the same disease within a week, urged Cuthbert to use that week to learn from him. 'What is the best book to study?' asked Cuthbert. 'St John the Evangelist,' Boisil answered. Bede, the historian of the early English Church, tells us these two students of John's Gospel dealt not with the profound arguments, but with the simple thing of 'the faith which works by love'.[1]

In manuscripts, John was depicted in the symbol of an eagle. Of all the living creatures, only the eagle can look straight into the sun and not be dazzled; likewise, John, of all the New Testament writers, has the most penetrating gaze into the eternal secrets in the heart of God. John, alone among the Gospel writers, gives an account of the things Jesus did at the beginning of his ministry before he went to Galilee. John alone tells us about intimate occasions at which he must have been present, and with which the Celtic Christians felt a deep rapport: the wedding reception at Cana (John 2:1–11 – the Celts loved celebrations of the extended family); the night visit to Jesus of the local councillor Nicodemus (3:1–15 – the Celts loved to bring local rulers to believe in Jesus); Jesus' meeting with the woman at the well in Samaria (John 4 – the Celtic monks, too, were liberated and transforming in their relationships with women); the raising from death of Lazarus in the family home (John 11 – the Celts also prized hospitality and raised people from death); Jesus' tender washing of the disciples' feet (John 13:1–17 – Celtic Christians made a practice of lovingly washing the feet of others); the sustenance of physical contact between Jesus and John at the Last Supper (John 13:23 – the Celts affirmed and were at home with the body); Jesus' extended teaching on the Holy Spirit and the Trinity (John 14–17 – for the Celts, the Trinity was the focus of everything); and Jesus' dying bestowal of his mother to the loved disciple, and through him, to the household of the early Church (John 19:25–7 – Mary remained a cherished part of the Celtic household of faith).

No wonder that the Celts' early medieval theologian, John Scotus Eriugena, wrote of John:

> [He] leans on the bosom of the Lord, which is the sacrament of contemplation, while [Peter] often hesitates, which is the symbol of restless action.[2]

Some time after the Church was established in Jerusalem, John went to apostle churches in the region around Ephesus, where he died a very old man. This was an area with a very different culture to the Jewish heartlands, and the key issue for them was this: Did they have to abandon their own culture and to adopt alien Jewish habits in order to be Christ-like Christians and churches, to the extent that they could no longer be at home with themselves?

Or did Christ want to incarnate his eternal presence in them as authentically, and therefore as originally, as he had in the Christians of Judea?

It is John who, in the prologue to his Gospel, portrays Christ as the One who created and sustains the whole universe, and who is the light of every person who comes into the world. That is one reason why the Celts blessed everything in creation. A famous story about John, which Cassian brought from the east when he came to live in Gaul, suggests yet another reason why the animal-loving Celts so took to John. One day, John was found playing with a tame partridge. A rather narrow-minded brother rebuked him for wasting time in this way. John replied: 'The bow that is always bent will soon cease to shoot straight.'

John's disciples come to Gaul

It is likely that evangelists from the area apostled by John founded the second-century lively Christian community in Lyons, Gaul, and that its first leader, Pothinus, knew John. Pothinus, along with many fellow Christians, died a beautiful martyrdom during a persecution in the year 177. The following year, Irenaeus became the leader of this community.

As a youth, Irenaeus sat at the feet of John's great friend, the saintly Polycarp, whom John appointed leader of the church in Smyrna. Polycarp used to recount his conversations with John, and he quoted from John's letter that he wrote in order to counter heresies. When Polycarp visited the leader of the church in Rome to sort out divergent dates for the keeping of Easter, it was agreed that the churches of the east should continue to follow the practice that John had always followed. On his return, Polycarp was arrested, and threatened with death by burning unless he recanted his faith in Christ. His famous reply, which preceded his noble death in 155, was: 'Eighty-six years have I served him, and he has done me no wrong: how then can I blaspheme my King who saved me?'[3]

Irenaeus travelled to Rome to study and was then ordained. He became a great Christian teacher and writer, who belonged to both the eastern and western churches. He remained the leader of the church in Lyons for twenty-two years. This may have been the main centre for Christianity in Gaul, which had links with the Celtic fringe of the Empire.

At a time when the Church throughout the west was moulded by the mind-set of the Greek world – which separated the spiritual from the material – Irenaeus fostered in the west a Christian community that kept alive John's spirituality of wholeness. Irenaeus believed that God became human so that humans may share in the life of God; that God's presence vibrates through every part of creation; and that Jesus and the Holy Spirit are the two hands of God.

It was Irenaeus who gave one of the first explicit expressions of the Trinity, based on his knowledge of the apostles.[4] It was Irenaeus who, captured by the wonder of Christ's incarnation, taught that 'the glory of God is seen through a human life fully lived'. In 190, Irenaeus intervened in the controversy about the date and manner of celebrating Easter. The Asiatic churches, including Rome, followed John's practice. They regarded Easter as the anniversary of Christ's death and kept a fast even if this fell on a Sunday. In 189, Victor, Bishop of Rome, talked of ex-communicating the Asiatics who insisted on this custom, but Irenaeus talked him out of it. Unity was central to him.[5]

Perhaps something of that heritage rubbed off on people like Hilary, who became Bishop of Poitiers in 353; and his convert-colleague Martin, who founded a Christ-like Christian community at Tours, which influenced many visitors from Britain. Certainly there was a new vision, also arising from the east, which began to grip the Christians in the Celtic fringe of the west. It was the vision of holy men and women creating communities of light in the eastern deserts.

During persecution many Christians from Gaul sought shelter in the western fringes of Britain, and vice versa, and the faith spread as a result of these movements.

One Christian in Lyons wrote the biography of Germanus, one of Gaul's outstanding Christian leaders, who came to Britain on two extended missions in the early part of the fifth century. It is possible that two Christian pioneers, Illtyd, the ex-soldier hermit of Wales, and Patrick, who evangelised Ireland, were his pupils, and he founded or inspired a wave of Christian communities.

The ill-fated rebellion by the British chief Constantine in 441 against the Saxon mercenaries who had been invited to help the British defend themselves, led to a mass exodus of Britons to Gaul. There were so many of them, and such a high proportion of Christians, that Mansuetus was appointed 'Bishop of the British'.

Although the famous battle of Badon, in about 490, which

some believe was led by Arthur, repulsed the pagan invaders, the aftermath was moral and social disintegration. The Church, too, seemed a spent force, though holy monks and hermits kept lone flames burning in the Celtic fringes. From this soil arose a home-grown Christian prophet, Gildas, whose writings have come down to us as *The Ruin of Britain*. This prophetic call (in about 540), to repent before God's judgement descended, was heeded by many.

Meanwhile, other links with the east were being forged. Trade routes between British ports and those of Constantinople and Alexandria were revived in the fifth century following the collapse of inland infrastructures. The Irish annal, the Book of Leinster, mentions seven monks from Egypt who died while visiting Ireland. Irish high crosses, and the Stowe Missal (the worship book of the monastery at Stowe) depict St Antony and St Paul of Thebes from Egypt. Nowhere else in western Europe are there exquisitely carved high standing crosses such as can be found in Ireland, west Wales and some of the Scottish islands. The nearest comparable work is in Armenia, 400 miles to the east. Dublin archaeologist Hilary Richardson asserts: 'alone in the Christian world, the extreme west and extreme east preserved an established convention of erecting monuments in stone'.[6]

A recent study of the hermit life in early Syrian Christianity yields interesting parallels to the Celtic west.[7] Some of the Celtic Christian artwork without doubt derives from the east. Illustrations in Celtic manuscripts like the *Book of Kells* (the illustrated copies of the Gospels which were perhaps produced by monks at Kells in the seventh or eighth century) resemble icons from Egypt and Syria. Each of the *Lindisfarne Gospels* (the beautifully illustrated copies of the four Gospels inscribed by monks at Lindisfarne in the eighth century) is introduced by a portrait of their author, in the Byzantine style. This was perhaps based on a Neapolitan manuscript brought to Lindisfarne in 688 by Theodore the Greek, who later became Archbishop of Canterbury.[8]

The circulation of books also linked the new wave of spiritual life in the eastern deserts with the Celtic Church. Some of the monks and nuns of the eastern deserts were scholars. The large, scattered community around Scete had access to a library, and the scrolls moved around. Athanasius' biography of St Antony, the early desert hermit, was read in Britain. Cassian's *Dialogues* (c A.D. 400) lit up the west with the holiness of the east. Nora

Chadwick concludes: 'We must postulate a strong intellectual influence operating on our islands from the East Mediterranean . . . There can be little doubt that it was mainly through books that knowledge came to Ireland from the Eastern Church, and that it was through books that they acquired their anchorite discipline from the East.'[9]

The eastern connection, through Gaul, is present in the founding of the first Christian communities in Britain. Ninian was fired by his time with Martin of Tours to found the 'Shining House' at Whithorn, in Galloway, in 398. Publicius, whose mother, Helen, had often entertained Martin at the court of her husband, the Emperor Magnus Maximus, is said to have founded the first monastery in Wales in 390. Illtyd, who founded Wales' great fifth-century monastic school at Llantwit Manor (or Llaniltud), near Coatbridge, is said to have spent time at Cassian's community at Marseilles.

There is a saying that Peter is the patron saint of the Roman Church; Paul is the patron saint of the Protestant Church; and John is the patron saint of the eastern and Celtic Churches. Christians in each tradition accept the teaching of all the apostles, but the Church is like a stool that needs three legs. The third leg, that of John, needs to be restored and given its full weight. 'The ancient cross on the Holy Isle of Iona was a Celtic Cross, with a circle, the symbol of Jesus' resurrection. It was the cross of St John, whose teaching stressed eternal life by way of the Cross' (Edward Samson). That is the dimension we must now restore.

A Prayer

> I muse on the eternal Logos of God, and
>   all creation is lit up:
> I muse on the eternal Light, and
>   every person is lit up:
> I muse on the eternal Life, and God's
>   heaven is lit up:
> I muse on the beloved disciple at the Last Supper and God's
>   sacrament is lit up:
> I muse on the loved mother and apostle at the cross and Christ's
>   church is lit up:
> I muse on the risen Christ at Lake Galilee and all our
>   Easters are lit up:
> I muse on the eternal Lamb of God, and eternity's tenderness
>   is lit up:
> I muse on the radiance of the eastern light, and pray that it
>   becomes the transforming glory of the west.

A Response

> I will ever contemplate that tender love, that deathless vision,
> that flowing life that John the loved disciple lived and fostered.

2

Communities of Faith

'All the believers continued together in close fellowship and shared their belongings with one another' (Acts 2:44).

Public life in recent decades has been dominated by the view that markets are the measure of all things. The rush towards unlimited consumer choice leads, inevitably, to the destruction of bonds based on non-material values. This trend is too powerful for any one political party to reverse: it is the motor of big business and media, yet it devastates family and destroys community. The modern technology of communication – cars, phones, fax, credit cards – means that I shop, meet, learn and make recreation wherever I fancy, regardless of who is my neighbour. Ties of blood or place become marginal.

All this affects churches, too. On any Sunday, a potential church-goer now has a long list of options: to go to the boat or caravan, to friends or relatives, to sports or social functions that one or other of their home circle is involved in; to lie in and watch a religious television programme, or to attend an interesting service that another church has advertised. The choice of a local church will itself be dictated by the consumer mentality: 'If I like the style of a church's music, leader, buildings, children's or after-care services, I will attend. If I grow tired of it, or if something better starts up at another church, or if something I don't like occurs, I will shop around again for another church. Whatever happens, I will avoid commitments, for they reduce my options. My highest goal, perhaps unacknowledged or unexpressed, is maximum choice.'

Churches have responded, as so they should, to market forces. In fact, a key word in church growth circles is 'presentation'. Churches become centres, like concert halls, that make attractive presentations. They are 'pick-up points'. This is excellent as far as it goes. Yet mere 'pick-up points' are not churches, for the church is the body of Christ, a community where each person is a member one of another. Churches have fallen for 'short-termism'; they have become a mirror image of society. However, since society itself is deeply diseased, these churches cannot offer a cure; they cannot model an alternative way.

The need for an alternative model is enormous. A huge part of the nation's health bill seems to be linked to the dis-ease and anxiety that consumerism produces. The value of community is immeasurable; yet as the experience of community vanishes, the longing for it increases. Is it possible for a comfortable, wealthy society to revolve around God? Is it possible to create models of an alternative society?

Unfortunately, the model of the medieval monastery rarely connects with contemporary longings for community. The traditional monasteries became enclosed, and remote from the people, no longer part of the warp and weft of local life. They began poor, but became comfortable. They began in simplicity, but became repositories of status. They began with liturgy in a popular idiom, but grew out of touch with the heart-language of popular culture. They began with monks and nuns who were vulnerable; but often these same people became defensive, and sometimes even oppressive. These monasteries began with the ideal of hospitality, but became less welcoming than the YMCA hostel or the Salvation Army soup kitchen. They began as places where all that is human in their members could flower; yet they became places where members felt trapped, and their personalities regressed. In short, the monasteries of the Roman Church became too static and over-institutionalised.

The Protestant criticism of monasteries was in part justified, because of these abuses, but it had a flawed theology. Dietrich Bonhoeffer deals with the Protestant doctrine of 'the invisible Church' in his treatise on the Sermon on the Mount. He points out that the call of Jesus to his disciples was to a visible community; flight into the invisible is a denial of the call.[1] Bonhoeffer believed that the renewal of the western Church could only come out of a new monasticism; and that the only thing the new monasticism would have in common with the old was the Sermon on the Mount. The spirit of our age may be summed up as, 'How happy are those who increase their power to consume'. The Sermon on the Mount may be summed up as, 'How happy are those who know they have nothing, theirs is the Kingdom of God'.

Models of community

So the need of today is for contemporary models of Christian community that grow, neither out of the mind-set of modern society nor out of that of the medieval Church, but out of our Christian roots. Where can these roots be found? To answer this we need to look at various models:

1 *Community of prophets model*. We learn of a group of prophets under the leadership of Elisha who had outgrown their base (2 Kings 6:1–3), so they went to a forest and built more cells out of the felled trees. This community is rooted in the commitment to listen to God and to respond in whatever way is appropriate. There is a pilgrim nature about it. The community moves with God, but it is not static.

2 *Apostolic model*. Jesus spent three years sharing his life with twelve men and some women helpers. They had no single base, though they had a network of homes – of relatives (e.g. Peter's in-laws) and of friends (e.g. Lazarus, Mary and Martha); they sometimes went away to mountain retreats. Their bond was the call to a common task which required total commitment to God and to one another.

3 *Jerusalem model*. The original Church in Jerusalem was a community. It met for daily prayer and Eucharist. Goods were shared in common. After persecution, however, this community had to disperse.

4 *Desert Fathers and Desert Mothers model*. The Celtic Church was deeply influenced by the movement that began in the Egyptian and Syrian deserts as a reaction against the laxity that had crept into the Church. In 305, St Antony began to organise this movement of Christians into the deserts of Egypt. These 'Desert Christians' sought to come closer to God by seeking him in remote and solitary places, far away from the temptations and corruption of worldly power. In this they felt they were following the example of Jesus, who had sometimes gone on his own to pray on the mountainside, away from his disciples and the crowds. However, like Jesus, they

did not become isolated. In time there were whole clusters of solitaries and even families. At Skete, many had their own huts and work, but they were linked by common values, occasional hospitality, and Sunday Eucharists. This movement caught the imagination of many devout people throughout the Christian world, but especially in the Celtic world.

A book about St Antony, written by Athanasius, fired the imagination of an officer named Martin in the Imperial Guard. He adopted the monastic ideal. When he was elected Bishop of Tours, in Gaul, he established a monastery in 371 whose aim was to be a colony, not of the debauched Empire, but of heaven. For Martin, a collection of hermits who were interested only in personal purity was not enough: they needed to model a new form of society. Geoffrey Ashe has written: 'Monks built a new society in the shell of the old. Here social distinctions were effaced, fresh scope was given to ability. Their community witnessed to the world's corruption . . . The monks built well enough to save Europe from total ruin.'[2] Young men of high and low birth poured into Tours to be trained by Martin. They went out owning nothing, fearing no one, loving God, winning souls. Among the young who came to learn from Martin was a Briton named Ninian.

Ninian arrived back in his native Galloway in 398, just twelve years before the last troops of the Roman Empire withdrew their protection of the native British from Anglo-Saxon invaders, and he established a hugely popular Christian community at Whithorn. Recent excavations have unearthed traces of this. Ninian recruited sons of leading families to a monastic school. This patterned a radical alternative to the superstitious and immoral ways of their world. The centre became known as 'Candida Casa' – Shining House. The same word was used in the Latin Bible to describe Jesus' transfiguration. Ailred, Ninian's biographer, tells us that all was love, there was nothing of fear in this 'radiant one'.[3] Although this wave of God was soon replaced by a wave of godless invaders, Ninian's work remained a beacon of hope for succeeding generations. In much of the Empire, the monasteries became more formal, but Ninian's centre remained a model of fellowship for countless groupings of monks, nuns and hermits throughout the Celtic lands.

Christianity was made the official religion of the Roman Empire in 386, although the organised Church in the cities tended to reflect rather than reform society. In 410, when the Goths sacked Rome, Jerome cried out: 'O weep for the Empire! Suddenly comes news of Rome's fall. The light of all the earth is extinguished.' Rome's fall had been made possible by the debauchery and corruption that had run rampant through the cities of the Empire. Yet in the darkness of collapse, Jerome sent out news of the beacon fires for Christ that remained alight in the deserts. Living at Bethlehem, Jerome helped keep the flame of holiness burning in the Christians of Gaul by giving them constant news of the lives of the monks in the desert caves of the Thebaid and of Nitria, through his courier Sysinus.

From Gaul, Bishop Germanus came to a debilitated church in Britain on two extended missions in 429 and 447. He encouraged the British Christians to follow the example of the Desert Fathers and Mothers; so many did this, that by the sixth century the primary expression of the Church was the monastic communities. Germanus ordained Illtyd who, like Martin, had renounced his life as a soldier in order to become a hermit. He became the founder of the monastery of Llan-Iltud (now Llantwit, near Coatbridge). Illtyd's monastery overflowed, not only with faith and prayer, but with good food and wine. It numbered among its disciples Malo, Samson, Teilo, Gildas, all of whom took the Christian faith to Brittany after the Saxons invaded Britain, where they founded monasteries, bishoprics and towns, some of which still bear their names.

When Samson was born in Wales in about 485, many clergy were lax and drunkards, but saints such as Illtyd and Bishop Dubricius transmitted the way of holiness through their monastic communities. The seventh-century biography of Samson, which includes eye-witness material handed down by his nephew, is one of the earliest records of life in Britain.[4]

Robert Van de Weyer writes:

> The heart of the Celtic fire was the monastery. The Celtic monastery was usually started by a hermit, who cleared a piece of forest and built himself a hut. Gradually others would come to join him, clearing some more woodland and erecting huts nearby. Then in their midst they would build a chapel, a simple wooden frame covered in turfs. Sometimes these communities grew to no more than ten or twenty people, but often they consisted of hundreds or even thousands of men and women, forming by far the largest settlements in the whole of the British

Isles. And they were constantly spawning new communities, as individual monks and nuns, weary of the bustle of the large monastery, went off into the forest to live as hermits; and soon others would come, to form another monastery.

In continental Europe . . . every aspect of a monk's life was governed by a strict Rule, and the abbot had absolute authority. In Britain and Ireland, by contrast, the monks and nuns enjoyed a high degree of freedom, and their way of life remained simple and flexible. They each worked out their own pattern of prayer and meditation, meeting only once a day for worship. The abbot was seen not as a ruler to whom obedience was owed, but rather as a wise spiritual guide from whom to seek advice . . . Every monastery had huts available for travellers and the sick; and the monks were expected to share with them some of the food they had gathered.[5]

In Ireland, monasteries were part of the homesteads and farms of extended families or even of whole clans, whose natural leaders became the spiritual leaders. Never have so many people in one country been formed in such a cradle of homely zeal. Vida D. Skudder has written:

In the main, no-one can doubt the surprising beauty of life in these centres of labour, learning and love. A few centuries later it is possible to claim that monasticism suppresses and belittles human nature; in the time of Bede its effect was to release and enrich. These Houses of Faith were centres of healthful democracy.

The monks cultivated and extended with enthusiasm all the knowledge and literature possessed by the world in their day. The distant places toward which they had first been led by a love of solitude, changed rapidly into cathedrals, cities, towns, or rural colonies, and served as centres, schools, libraries, workshops and citadels of the scarcely converted families . . .[6]

As Celtic monasticism overflowed its own territorial limits, and spread across the Continent, it seemed for a time that it would be the dominating ideal of later monasticism. However, the constitution of the communities founded by Columbanus was exclusive, and this was no doubt bound up with its missionary character. This was at once the cause of its temporary triumph and of its ultimate decay.

The crisis that befell the later forms of monasticism in the west were largely due, according to the Community of the Servants of the Will of God, which exists in Crawley Down, Sussex, 'to their failure to pass on the principles of Christian community life to the church at large. The result has been increasing individualism in the church which amounts to a heresy, and widespread social breakdown in the western world.'[7] Father Gregory, the prior of the Community of the Servants of the Will of God, says:

> God founds his church on both his apostles and his prophets. Not only on the apostles and their successors whose duty is to order the pastoral and worship life of the church, but also on the prophets, whom God raises up at will to recall the church to hear and obey the call of the Living God who leads his people on. The monastic life is meant to be such an organism within the church. In the West, however, we have tended to tame it and silence it by integrating it too closely into the institutions of the church. That has been self-destructive for the church.[8]

The new monasticism

In Part One of this book, I mentioned a vision of a large old oak tree in an apparently shapeless wood, which had been uprooted in a gale. As a group of landscape planners surveyed the scene, wondering about a replacement for the oak, a non-professional in the group spotted that there could be a spacious avenue, lined with young trees that were in fact already shooting up in the right places, although self-seeded. Even as some forms of traditional orders die, Thomas Merton's call for the development of new forms of contemplative apostolates, and of a monasticism that is open to the listening and pilgrimage of its members, and dialogue with society, speaks to our time.

Buds of the new monasticism that Bonhoeffer prophesied are beginning to appear, for example the Iona, the Northumbrian and the southern-based Othona Communities. John Skinner, father of four children, and a founder of the Northumbria Community, believes that the essence of monasticism is separation from status. Its essence used to be thought of as separation from a partner, possessions and private pursuits (vows of celibacy, poverty and obedience). However, those are *examples* of one way of living the monastic life; they are not the *only* way to live it. The impression has been given that there was only one form of monasticism, and that it distances monks from ordinary people.

In true monasticism, the opposite is true. It becomes a separation from everything that divides people – status, manipulation, possessive relationships or use of material things. It is possible to be married, or to be part of a local church community, and to live as a monk. One contemporary definition of a monk is: *one who separates from everybody in order to be united to everyone*.

New movements such as the Northumbria Community seek a redefinition of monasticism. The French Community of the Beatitudes, near Rouen, admit married novices, and the monastery includes children. In doing this, it helps to recover the sense that marriage is a vocation. This monastery, in common with other charismatic communities in France, is also rediscovering its Jewish roots.

In the light of his experience of L'Arche Communities, Jean Vanier has reflected upon some conditions that are necessary for true community to exist: willingness to be vulnerable; to know our limitations, weaknesses; to know and be known; to discover our deepest wounds; belonging; listening; being, contemplative prayer. A community has hospitality at its heart; a sect has exclusion at its heart. A leader of community sets members free to follow their own authentic Christ-centred journeys; the leader of a sect ties members ever more rigidly to the ways of its founder. A sect has control at its heart; a community has journey at its heart.[9]

Community is a place where everyone is allowed to be themselves; where we face the shadows in ourselves. My particular community is both the core group, and the larger community, or neighbourhood, in which it is set. Out of this grows a third sense of community – we belong to the land. There is a movement from egoism to outgoing unconditional love. Every member has a task.

A number of local churches now have a core of members who make vows, or subscribe to a Rule or Pattern of Life that enshrines these ideals. At its simplest, church members anywhere can take up the challenge to:

1 Pray together daily
2 Live simply
3 Make unity

Monasticism was not *a* feature of the Celtic Church, as it was generally in the western Church; it was *the* feature. In the same way, community has to become *the* mark of local churches and Christian groups today.

A Prayer

Sacred Three, you are community. Forgive our sin of denying your image in us. Lead us to those with whom you wish us to make community. Teach us to be true to the deepest things in ourselves, which will form natural bonds with the deepest things in others whom you similarly call. Call into being new communities of faith today.

A Response

I will seek to make community with other Christians, and to move towards a fuller sharing of myself, my time and my possessions.

3

People on the Move for God

'If you wander off the road to the right or the left, you will hear his voice behind you saying "Here is the road. Follow it"' (Isaiah 30:21).

'Three Irishmen came to King Alfred in a boat without any oars from Ireland, whence they had stolen away because they wished to go on pilgrimage for the love of God they cared not where.'[1] Those three monks were among the great number who for over a period of 500 years set out to wander across the face of Europe, from Iceland to Italy. They left homeland and friends, and all life's securities, in order that they might set out into the unknown, a journey for God. They were not tied to earthly securities. They did not get their adventure from intellectual exploration, but from obedience.

In this, they mirrored those personalities portrayed in the pages of the Book of Genesis who set out into the unknown in obedience to God. These biblical travellers did not, as we are prone to, try to ensure a good result before they set out. They achieved results not by going to people who were likely to react in a way that would bring the desired results, but through prayer.

The Irish monks, writes Shirley Toulson, 'seem to have taken the words of the second-century Irenaeus literally, when he defined the true search for God as starting from *apavia* (roadlessness), a state of complete trust in the direction of God rather than that of a human decision'.[2] 'I am always moving from the day of birth to the day of death', said Columbanus, who believed that 'Christians must travel in perpetual pilgrimage as guests of the world'. Likewise, 'Your feet will bring you to where your heart is', says one Irish proverb.

A fifth-century Irish manuscript, 'A Catalogue of the Saints of Ireland', arranged Irish saints into three orders. These were the Spirit-filled bishops of Patrick's time, priests of the following century who followed the example of people such as St David of Britain, and the Third Order who were holy people who wandered to remote places and had nothing of their own. Their ideal was to seek 'the places of one's resurrection'. This form of permanent exile from one's family, to pass one's life in solitude, was a feature of the anchorites, who had a rule of life but who were solitaries. The influence of these people, who harnessed a natural wanderlust to God, can hardly be over-estimated. David Edwards claims that it changed Europe.[3]

Nora Chadwick reminds us: 'One of the most striking and original features of Irish Christianity is the love of wandering . . ., which was interpreted in both its literal and its figurative sense.'[4] The epic stories of faith journeys came to have as much significance as the events themselves. 'In epic literature', John Sharkey writes, 'the journey is symbolic of the life of the soul, the cycle of experience it must undergo . . . The telling of our journeys is as much a religion as the ceremonies themselves.'[5]

The ninth- or tenth-century story of Brendan's voyage across the Atlantic in a tiny coracle captured the Celtic imagination:

> Brendan chose fourteen monks from his community and made this proposal to them. 'My beloved fellow soldiers in the spiritual war . . . I want to seek out the Island of Promise of which our forefathers have spoken. Will you come with me?' As soon as he had finished speaking the monks replied with one voice: '. . . we are ready to go with you, for better or worse, so long as it is God's will'.[6]

> For the next two weeks the wind was fair, so that they did no more than steady the sail. But then the wind fell, and they had to row, day by day. When their strength eventually failed, Brendan comforted them: 'Have no fear, brothers, for God is our captain, and our pilot; so take in the oars, and set the sail, letting him blow us where he wills'.[7]

Celtic Christians have retained this ability to sit loose to the ties that bind, and to follow their inspirations. The many journey prayers in the *Carmina Gadelica*, Alexander Carmichael's nineteenth-century collection of oral prayers from the western Isles and Highlands of Scotland, bear witness to this:

God be with thee in every pass,
Jesus be with thee on every hill,
Spirit be with thee on every stream,
Headland and ridge and lawn;

Each sea and land, each moor and meadow,
Each lying down, each rising up,
In the trough of the waves, on the crest of the billows,
Each step of the journey thou goest.[8]

However solitary the place to which they went, they knew they were never alone:

Saviour and friend, how wonderful art Thou!
My companion upon the changeful way.
The comforter of its weariness.
My guide to the eternal town.
The welcome at its gate.[9]

Today, people from the New World make reverse journeys to those made by the early Irish monks. Edward Sellner, in his book *Soul-making: The Telling of a Spiritual Journey*, describes how the 'Cuthbert figure' in his dreams was responsible for calling him back to the lands of the Celtic saints.[10]

We all have a journey to make. Jesus told us to pray 'Lead us not into temptation' (Luke 11:14). What are the places we should steer clear of? Places where the spirit of fear or lust rules, or that of artificiality, unbelief, or the power of one ego over another, or the shoddy? To know where we should *not* be led is an exploration in itself. Yet far bigger is to tread the way of the true journey; to pray 'lead us into your way, lead us to the kingdom of God, lead us into our place of resurrection'.

Leaving the past behind

Each one of us needs to identify in our own lives any place where we have given up thinking that change can come, and to seek God's guidance on how we can move on. Frequently we do not leave the past behind. We clasp on to it. We dissect it, and let fears for the future, tempered by the past, unconsciously prevent us from taking up the task eternal. We are tempted to go the known ways, the safe ways, basking in the achievements, perhaps, of forefathers in the faith, not replenishing spiritually or materially the capital they left to us.

Many people discount the possibility of being a person of pilgrimage because, they feel, they are trapped in an institution. Church leaders are no more exempt from this than are others. Yet it *is* possible. Archdeacon Michael Handley says that clergy in the 1960s and 1970s were motivated by social care, and that now that role has been taken away, nothing has taken its place – except greater ecclesiastical busyness. Archdeacon Handley realised he was being asked by the diocesan machine to do twenty-three sessions a week on 'machinery business'. Yet an inner voice was saying, 'All sessions belong to me and only twelve belong to the organisation as a matter of routine.'

Archdeacon Handley then went on a cycling pilgrimage through France to Santiago de Compostella. It took many days. A woman who asked him how long it took reflected: 'That's quite right. The nearer the centre you are the more you ought to do this sort of thing.' So now the archdeacon sets time aside to do 'useless things' (none of the twenty-three sessions were to do 'useless things'), to learn to play with time, to waste time for God; to kill the mentality of control. Once when he was on the way to a busy agenda, an inner voice said, 'Call at this house'. It turned out that a man had just died there. The archdeacon was able to help and pray with the relatives – then he left to carry on his business. But if he had not learned to set aside time for 'useless things', he would never have heard the inner voice.

Living off centre
> Like a wooden spinning top
> With its main mass lopsidedly near the edge,
> I have wobbled erratically
> Weaving an uncertain
> Inconsistent
> And unstable
> Course
> Through life so far.
>
> I have lived life inauthentically
> Off centre
> Away from the core of my being
> Not constantly tapping into the well
> Of my being.
> I have not invoked my vocational

Mystery, endowed by the Eternal One.
At an early age an obscuring
Of the centre, was made manifest.

Now in middle age, early forties
I want to spin, dance truly
From my centre,
So I am still, yet turning
to the Source of life within and beyond.[11]

A Prayer
Lead me from that which binds to that which frees;
Lead me from that which cramps to that which creates,
Lead me from that which lies to that which speaks truth,
Lead me from that which blights to that which ennobles.
Lead me from that which hides to that which celebrates;
Lead me from that which fades to that which endures.

A Response
I detach myself from dependency upon earthly securities and
will go wherever God leads.

4

Contemplative Prayer

'Pray without ceasing' (1 Thessalonians 5:17).

The theologian and historian Bede (*c* 673–735) tells us that during St Cuthbert's years at Old Melrose Monastery in the seventh century, it was his habit to go outside and spend the night in prayer, returning just in time for morning prayer with the other monks. During a visit to the nuns at Coldingham Convent, Cuthbert was seen praying in the sea up to his arms and neck in water, the splash of the waves accompanying his vigil throughout the dark hours of the night. At daybreak, two sea otters knelt on the sand and warmed his feet.

Many questing young people and stressed older people nowadays seek relaxation through meditation. They look for it in Hindu, Buddhist and other eastern religions. They are often surprised to learn that there is such a way within the Christian tradition, a way that is known as contemplation.

The techniques of these varying traditions can be similar, but the destination is different. 'For the easterner the goal is *nirvana*, which means "where there is no wind", and for us [Christians] the wind of the Spirit is vital, even when it blows harshly,' writes Madeleine L'Engle. 'We do not move from meditation into contemplation, into self-annihilation, into death, in order to be freed from the intolerable wheel of life. No. We move – are moved – into death in order to be discovered, to be loved into truer life by our Maker. To die to self in the prayer of contemplation is to move to a meeting of lovers.'[1] Celtic spirituality, which has contemplative prayer at its heart, has much to offer those who are questing; unfortunately, the ignorance of contemplative prayer by those Christians they know may prevent them from finding this hidden treasure.

Yet what is contemplative prayer? This question is frequently

asked by Christians who assume that the only 'real' prayer is intercession that requests God to do certain specific things. Christianity,
they believe, is about effective speaking or doing, and therefore
contemplative, or non-directed, prayer is at best marginal. Three
points need to be made in response to this misconception.

First, St Paul urges Christians to 'pray in all ways' (Ephesians
6:18). Thus to exclude contemplative prayer is to dismiss this
Scripture. Second, contemplative prayer is the opposite of con-
trolling prayer. It is fatally easy to project the unrecognised needs
of one's own ego into prayer requests. Prayer meetings or private
prayer times then become dominated by human self-will dressed
in religious clothing. Control is the last thing a Christian clings
to in her or his journey into obedience. Contemplative prayer is
natural, unprogrammed; it is perpetual openness to God, so that
in the openness his concerns can flow in and out of our minds as
he wills.

Third, research suggests that in any case contemplative (i.e.
non-directed) prayer may get better 'results' than directed prayer.
The Spindrift Organisation in Lansdale, Pennsylvania, has for
a decade studied the ability of praying persons (Christian and
non-Christian) to affect the behaviour of simple biological systems
– for example, the germination rate of seeds, the metabolic activity
of yeast cultures, as well as of human illnesses. They measured the
difference in results between directed prayer (e.g. when the person
asks for a specific result – for example, that a cancer will leave the
body) and non-directed prayer (when the praying person simply
asks God to do whatever is best). The Spindrift studies show that
though both approaches are effective, the non-directed approach
is quantitatively more effective.[2]

Contemplative prayer, or the prayer of the heart, was for
the desert Christians the only known way to meet a biblical
requirement. Jesus' injunction to 'pray always' (Luke 18:1) and
St Paul's injunction to 'pray without ceasing' (1 Thessalonians
5:17) cannot be literally fulfilled solely by having 'prayer times'
or 'prayer meetings' – valuable though these can be. They can
only be fulfilled when 'all the movements of the heart become a
single-hearted and uninterrupted prayer'.[3] Prayer then becomes
an inner disposition that is present in every activity of life; it becomes
a love that always tends towards its Beloved even when it must
attend to something else.

Contemplative prayer is the enjoyment of being alone with God.

Yet contemplatives are realists. The person who communes with the heart of Jesus is in communion with the heart of the world. Thus those who spend much time in silence find themselves closer to people than if they were physically together. Contemplative prayer takes the psychic energy that human nature usually expends on a myriad of surface things – chatter or cooking, committees or communications, conflicts or career – and offers it to God.

The Celts were natural contemplatives, and hermits, pilgrims and heroes sought out rugged peninsulas or hidden woodland glades in order to be alone with God. Many active church leaders also sought out lonely places during Lent or Advent for periods of fasting and prayer. In Irish monasteries it became the practice for some of the monks to withdraw from community life for a time and to go into some nearby forest or cave. These places often became known as 'deserts', and names like Dysart, Disert, Diarmada and Desertoghill still recall what once were the dwellings of solitaries.

Much of the inspiration for contemplative prayer came from the Fathers and Mothers of the eastern deserts, and the Christian Celts were magnetised by their example. At the start of their experiment in prayer, the desert Christians, especially those who were younger, had to use repeated repetition of a few words, in order to move their centre of attention from the world to God. The 'Jesus Prayer' became almost a norm: 'Lord Jesus Christ, have mercy on me a sinner'. They were practical people, and so they would repeat this while they sat at a table making mats out of palm leaves which they would sell to make their living. Gradually, the need for words faded as their hearts, hands and heads became purified and united – 'a flame for God', as they would say.

The idea of incessant prayer is a constant refrain in the sayings of the Desert Fathers, collections of which were made. 'Enter into your heart and stay there' was one of the sayings.[4] John Cassian (AD 360–435), who journeyed from the Egyptian desert to popularise its spirituality in Gaul, described the gradual purifying that came to the prayer of the desert Christians:

> It reaches out beyond all human feelings. It is neither the sound of the voice nor the movements of the tongue nor articulated words. The soul, bathed in light from on high, no longer uses human speech, which is always inadequate. Like an overabundant spring, all feelings overflow and spring

forth towards God at the same time. In this short moment, it says so many things that the soul, once it has recovered itself, could neither express nor go over them in its memory.[5]

Patrick, who as a slave spent enforced solitude tending the sheep on the Antrim hills, followed the example of the desert Christians. To begin with he had to work at saying prayers, and indeed he later taught all his followers to repeat frequently the prayer 'Lord have mercy'. Eventually, prayer became second nature to him:

More and more did my love of God, and my awe of him and faith increase. My spirit was moved so that in a single day I would say as many as a hundred prayers and in the night a like number, even when I was staying in the woods and on the mountain. And I used to rise before dawn for prayer, in snow and frost and rain, and I used to feel no ill effect and there was no slackness in me. I now realise it was because the Spirit was glowing in me.[6]

Later in his life Patrick had a vision of someone praying inside his body. Then God revealed to him that it was the Spirit praying in him. When he woke up, Patrick remembered St Paul's words that 'the Spirit pleads for us with groanings beyond words' (Romans 8:26). Praying in tongues can be another form of contemplative prayer.

Columba often felt the need to go away to a place to be alone. Sometimes in the night he would go to the church to pray, and when in Skye he went into dense forest to pray by himself. And in Iona, 'he went to seek a place remote from men and fitting for prayer', says Adamnan.[7] This was perhaps the Hermit's Cell, whose foundations may still be seen in a lonely glen leading to Iona's western shore.

Cuthbert, as we have learned, prepared for his long teaching, healing and evangelistic journeys by spending whole nights in prayer, sometimes immersed in the sea. When he was based at Lindisfarne he waded out to what is still called Cuthbert's Isle to commune with God in the harmony of sea and sky. At the end of his life, alone on the Inner Farne Island, Bede tells us 'Cuthbert finally entered into the remoter solitude he had so long sought, thirsted after, and prayed for. He was delighted that after a long and spotless active life he should be thought worthy to ascend to the stillness of Divine contemplation.'[8]

Nora Chadwick writes: 'The Christianity of the Celts had a marked spirituality of its own. Having no towns, no currency, no large-scale industries, it had little temptation to material and worldly ideals. It retained to the end a serene inner life which could never be repeated in a rapidly changing world, and it could convey this spirit in its poetry at home and abroad to after ages in its work and in its religious devotions.'[9]

But can mobile, urban people enter into contemplative prayer? The deep need for this in the human soul, which has been repressed for so long, is now making itself felt as much in towns as in the countryside. There is a mushrooming of prayer corners in houses, prayer cells in gardens, or poustinias (rooms or houses set aside for quiet or prayer) for general use in the grounds of monasteries or landowners. I hope that a further development will be the provision of soundproofed cubicles in places of work. Steve Goodwin, a contemplative and iconographer from Birmingham, is seeking to draw together a network of contemplatives in inner-city areas. Deserts, silences and solitudes are not necessarily places, but states of mind and heart. Centres of silence may be found in cities; still pools in trains and plains; prayer corners in houses or storerooms.

> The world gives itself up to incessant activity merely because it knows nothing better. The inspired person works among its whirring wheels also, but he knows whither the wheels are going. For he has found the centre where all is stillness.
>
> (Paul Brenton)

> There is all the difference in the world between an unsought loneliness and a sought solitude.
>
> (Roland Walls)

> In every one lies a zone of solitude that no human intimacy can fill; and there God encounters us.
>
> (Brother Roger of Taizé)

> There is a contemplative in all of us,
> almost strangled but still alive,
> who craves quiet enjoyment of the Now
> and longs to touch the seamless
> garment of silence
> which makes us whole.
>
> *(Alan P. Torey)*

A Prayer

Lord, you are my island, in your bosom I rest.
You are the calm of the sea, in that peace I lie.
You are the deep waves of the ocean,
In their depths I stay.
You are the silence of the spheres, in that space I live.
You are the smooth white strand of the shore,
In its swell I sing.
You are the ocean of life that laps my being.
You are the Lord of my life,
In you is my eternal joy.[10]

A Response

I will cherish the place of inner silence where God and I can
commune in intimacy.

**A cell of Celtic monks on the island of Inchcolm in the
Firth of Forth**

5

Rhythm in Work and Worship

'Day by day they met as a group in the Temple' (Acts 2:46).

The first Christians naturally adopted a rhythm of daily prayer and of weekly celebration of the Lord's Supper. They, like Jesus, were Jews. Their Scriptures revealed that God expressed rhythm in his universe; in the seven 'days' of creation (Genesis 1 and 2), in the seasons, and in the cycle of each day. They were familiar with the custom of prayer at dawn, noon and dusk (Psalm 55:17), and even of prayer seven times a day (Psalm 119:164). They knew that fields must lie fallow in order to remain fruitful, and they used the same word, 'sabbath', for both a year of rest for fields and a day of rest for people (Leviticus 25). Jesus echoed this in his pattern of work followed by withdrawal, as did his disciples.

Unfortunately, when the Church became so successful that it 'embellished' rather than redeemed the greedy restlessness of the world, it lost touch with God's rhythms at the still centre of the world. Yet mercifully, the Christians who moved out of the urban rat-race into the desert places soon restored a rhythm of prayer, work, study and rest.

The rural Celts never lost touch with the rhythms of the 'still centre', and the pattern that marked the monasteries of the east was a hallmark of the whole Celtic Church. Today, people are growing sick of the frenetic dis-eased western lifestyle. Research suggests that there is an imprint in every soul that reflects universal rhythms; once again, ordinary people seek to tune their lives to these, but the rhythms too must be redeemed.

Columba's monastery on Iona exemplified a rhythm of work and worship: 'The days were filled with prayer, study, and manual labour . . . in dairy, granary, or in the fields, each worshipped God in his appointed task, and made his toil a sacramental thing . . . The secret of the early Celts lay in this, that they linked sacrament with service, altar with hearth, worship with work.'[1]

It is important that we too discover the rhythm of praying through our work, and sometimes a simple manual task can even assist the praying heart in its focus. Prayer-baskets were woven simply out of reeds as monks framed their prayers. Thus the simplest task can become for us a 'prayer-basket':

> It's when we give you a helping hand
> we meet you, Lord of sea and land.
> Ebb tide, full tide,
> Let life's rhythms flow.
> Full tide, ebb tide,
> How life's beat must go.[2]

The early Celtic Church observed the rhythm of sabbath (i.e. Saturday) rest as well as worship on Sunday. The Irish *Senchus Mor* were Christianised Brehon laws believed to have been framed with the help of Patrick. They required that every seventh day should be devoted to the service of God, in terms of both tithes and time. Columba's Rule stipulated that the special food allowance to mark Sunday should also be given on Saturday 'because of the reverence that was paid to the Sabbath in the Old Testament. It differs from Sunday in work only.'[3] Adamnan, Columba's biographer, treated the sabbath with a respect that was to disappear in succeeding generations. The Celtic Church was following Jewish and eastern patterns in this matter. Gradually, Romanising influences, which were not without an anti-Semitic and an urban mentality, and that were divorced from the land, enforced Sunday, not Saturday, as the rest day, and Saturday became secularised.

There was also a rhythm throughout the week. The Iona practice, which Aidan continued at Lindisfarne, was to abstain from daylight meals on Wednesdays and Fridays. This custom was followed by 'many devout men and women who were inspired to follow his example', though the rule of hospitality meant that this practice could be waived in honour of guests. Columba and Patrick seem to have treated Thursday as a regular day for special devotion.[4]

Seasons

The rhythm of the church year, with its great feasts of Pentecost, Christmas and Easter, preceded by fifty-three days of fasting, meant much to the Celts. The controversy (referred to in Part Two, Chapter 1) over Easter is complicated. The problem may simply have been that the Celts failed to update their dating system in line with wider church changes because they were cut off from communications. Yet I suspect this issue has also to do with rhythm. Leslie Hardinge succeeds in throwing light on this subject in chapter 5 of his book *The Celtic Church in Britain*.[5] The eastern churches were periodically at odds with Rome over the method of deciding the date of Easter. They had a sympathy with the Jewish rhythm, which related Passover to the waning and waxing of the moon. The Roman approach was to use a method that was administratively and symbolically convenient. Over the years, various adjustments were agreed at different councils, though there were disagreements among churches themselves in different regions, including the Celtic lands.

Days to commemorate special events were celebrated. Highlights were the Easter Eve Fire vigil, the transfiguration, the return of the holy family from Egypt, and a number of feasts to do with the family life of Christ. And there were the beginnings of days to honour the great saints of God. The author of the *Life of Samson of Dol* writes: 'To honour the festivals of the saints is nothing else than to adjust lovingly our mind to their good qualities . . . so that by imitating them we may be able to follow the same men, under God's guidance . . .'[6]

One thing that destroys rhythm in worship is an insensitive centralisation that is alien to the locality. We know that worship in the Celtic Church was at first free from this sort of centralisation, because there are records of the later imposition of Roman usage. On the Continent, Boniface imposed uniformity upon churches with Celtic foundations in 817, but the islands of Britain and Ireland were left to themselves a little longer. In Ireland it was not until the twelfth century that Bishop Malachy of Armagh imposed a uniform Roman liturgy, and the papal legate, the Bishop of Limerick, required that all previous usages 'give place to one Catholic and Roman Office'.[7]

The Celtic model is surely appropriate for our plural, 'pick 'n' mix' culture. Jeremy Fletcher, reporting on a day on Worship and Computers, organised by the liturgical exploration group, Praxis, writes:

> In a non-book, image-centred, multi-media culture, can we afford not to use the presentational possibilities computers afford us? Similarly, the global exchange of information now available through computers is a root attack on centralisation. Computers give access to huge resources, with the ability to customise them for local use, in a way not possible before. Perhaps we are heading to a time like the pre-print days, where there were local groups of rites, rather than one central authorised one.[8]

The Celtic churches also retained a rhythm of heritage. They drew on eastern, Gallican and Roman liturgies. They generally used Latin, which was the legacy that the departing civil servants of the Empire bequeathed to the centres of learning, which were the monasteries and churches. We can hardly imagine, however, that they used anything other than the vernacular when they gathered for informal occasions in the open air. The Druid bards were adept at singing in the language of the people, and it is likely that the Christians maintained this practice.

The experience of Caedmon, the cowherd at Whitby monastery, suggests that the Christian communities were the primary focus for local celebrations, and the local language would certainly have been used. Columba composed over three hundred songs; these, too, were probably not all in Latin.

Another thing that destroys grassroots rhythm in worship is proud, or contrived, triumphalism. A number of remarkable archaeological finds give us an idea of what kinds of vessel were used for the bread and wine at the Eucharist. Up to the fourth century, ordinary vessels used in the home were used in worship; they breathe the air of simplicity. Eighth-century Irish chalices found at Ardagh and Derry have developed a beauty and elegance that speak of heart-felt, not forced, devotion.[9]

The worship of the Celts was scriptural, liturgical, varied. It had spontaneity; it was eucharistic; and it was rooted in an intense communion. In Ireland, baptism was normally by immersion, preceded by instruction. Valuing the apostle's observation that Christians 'are buried with Christ' in baptism, the Irish theologians understood that 'three waves pass over us in

baptism, because he was three days in the sepulchre', hence
they dipped the person in the water three times. Instruction,
belief in God, repentance, grief of heart and penance were
prerequisites of baptism in the Church of Patrick's Ireland.[10]
In Britain, these customs may have prevailed in the lifetime of
Patrick's parents, but the issue of indiscriminate infant baptism
soon raised its head. It seems that they blessed babies in the
early days, but later they were told not to refuse to baptise
any baby.

Celtic worship has a rhythm of silence and reflection, especially
during seasons of fasting, vigils, and days like Good Friday. The
Desert Fathers took years to live one word. Brother Roger of
the Taizé community understands why we must rekindle this. He
has written: 'Since the sixteenth century, words have gradually
invaded churches, to such an extent that the worship of the People
of God risks being an intellectual exercise rather than radiant
Communion.'[11]

There is also the rhythm of poetry in Celtic worship. A friend
and I were trying to translate the Latin of the Stowe Missal (the
worship book of the monastery at Stowe). Since his Latin, though
better than mine, was not fluent, we finished with a far from
exact translation. We found, however, that the poetry of words
and phrases in the Missal caused our imaginations to soar, and
inspired the writing of a Eucharist in the Celtic tradition whose
Prayer of Thanksgiving concludes:

> Risen Christ, we welcome you. You are the flowering bough
> of creation; from you cascades music like a million stars, truth
> to cleanse a million souls. From you flee demons, omens and
> ill-will; around you rejoice the angels of light. Father, send us
> the tender Spirit of the Lamb; feed us with the Bread of Heaven;
> may we become drunk with your holiness.[12]

> Ebb tide, full tide, praise the Lord of land and sea;
> **Barren rocks, and darting gulls, praise his holy name!**
> Poor folk, royal folk, praise the Lord of land and sea;
> **Pilgrimed sands, sea-shelled strands, praise his holy name!**
> Fierce lions, gentle lambs, praise the Lord of land and sea;
> **Noble women, mission priests, praise his holy name!**
> Chanting boys, slaves set free, praise the Lord of land and
> sea;
> **Old and young and all the land, praise his holy name!**[13]

A Prayer
> Early in the morning I wait on you, O Lord;
> Day by day I toil for you, O Lord;
> At the bright noon-day I recollect you, O Lord;
> In talk and recreation I enjoy you, O Lord;
> In study and in prayer I learn of you, O Lord;
> At nightfall and in sleep I rest in you, O Lord.

A Response
> I will make a plan for personal and corporate prayer, for spaces, and for marking special days, that is true to the deepest rhythms of my life and of all life.

6

Holy Places: Healed Land

'Take off your sandals, because you are standing on holy ground' (Exodus 3:5).

The 'holy place', which is a meeting place with God, is a recurring theme in Scripture. Each of the patriarchs set up altars in places where God had met with them in a special way. These were usually made of stone. The prophet Elijah restored the altar of God that had stood on Mount Carmel, but had been demolished (1 Kings 18:30). Names were given to these places that reflected the experience that had taken place; for example, Bethel (House of God) – so named by Jacob after his vision of God there (Genesis 28:11–12).

When God chose a people, he said, 'I will give you the land' (Genesis 35:12). Each tribe, each household, was allocated a piece of God's earth. In the Bible, place is linked to God's calling of people. Only from the security of a safe place can we move out into the endless horizons of God's universe, and into eternity.

Jesus had special meeting places with God. Sometimes these were in the desert, at other times they were on a mountainside. Likewise, the Celtic Christians had special places in the rocky peninsulas or forests that served as deserts for them. Jesus also had special places for meeting God's friends. For example, he told his disciples that after his resurrection he would go to Galilee where they were to meet him (Matthew 26:32; 28:10,16).

At the root of the idea of holy places is the incarnation of God in a particular person, in a particular place, at a particular time. Christianity is not just a set of spiritual ideas; it is anchored in what God has done in history. This principle does not only apply to the supreme point in history – the first Easter in

Jerusalem – it also applies at points throughout history. So if an apostle plants a work of God in a place, it becomes a little Jerusalem.

Celtic Christians made places holy, and they were always on the look-out for their own 'place of resurrection'. Patrick Thomas has written:

> It is this ability to fuse together the unique time and place of Christ's birth in Bethlehem with our own specific present here in Wales or Ireland or Scotland which is part of the genius of Celtic spirituality; a realisation that the eternal moments of the Incarnation or the Crucifixion or the Resurrection can transcend time and space, enabling us to relocate Bethlehem or Calvary or the Garden of the Third Day in our own back yard.[1]

Thomas quotes the modern Welsh poet D. Gwenault Jones, who well captures this incarnational approach: 'And what is more Cardiff is as close as Calvary, and Bangor every inch as Bethlehem. The storms are stilled on Cardigan Bay, and on every street the lunatics are healed by the edge of his hem.'

A sense of place seems to be a necessary factor in psychological well-being. The Swiss doctor Paul Tournier, in his book *A Place for You*, concludes that 'to exist is to have a place'.[2] A sense of place, although it is dulled in our materialistic society, seems also to be a primal, God-given instinct that has decisively shaped civilisations. In the rites of the cave we find

> the social and religious impulses that conspired to draw men finally into cities, where the original feelings of awe, reverence, pride and joy would be further magnified . . . The first germ of the city is in the meeting place that serves as the goal for pilgrimage: a site to which groups are drawn back because it concentrates, in addition to any natural advantages it may have, certain 'spiritual' or supernatural powers.[3]

Today, a longing is resurfacing to make blighted places holy, and for once-hallowed places to come again into their own:

> Land of my Fathers
> how I long to return, to touch thy earth,
> and find thy sacred paths,
> well-walked with the Gospel of Peace,
> veiled now in the shadow of mediocrity (John T. Skinner).

The Celtic world of Britain, Ireland and Brittany is dotted with holy places. Two of its most holy places are Iona and Lindisfarne. Iona, the island Columba made into a beacon for Christ, was also home to Aidan and Oswald. It was known as 'a thin place', because, it was said, the space between heaven and earth there was 'thin'. Fiona Mcleod has written:

A few places in the world are to be held holy, because of the great love which consecrates them and the faith which enshrines them. One such is Iona . . . It is but a small isle, fashioned of a little sand, a few grasses salt with the spray of an ever-restless wave, a few rocks that wade in heather, and upon whose brows the sea-wind weaves the yellow lichen. But since the remotest days, sacrosanct men have bowed here in worship. In this little island a lamp was lit whose flame lighted pagan Europe. From age to age, lowly hearts have never ceased to bring their burden here. And here Hope waits. To tell the story of Iona is to go back to God, and to end in God.[4]

Lindisfarne, the cradle of Christianity for much of England, eventually became known as Holy Island, and multitudes have come as pilgrims to this home of Aidan, Cuthbert and their brothers in Christ. In the visitors' book at Marygate House, Lindisfarne, these words are inscribed:

> Primeval fire fused a cradle of rock:
> Born by the rocking tides,
> Smooth sand folded its hollows.
>
> Frail seeds flew
>   on the wind's shoulders;
> Blessed by the soft rain
>   and warmth of sun
> Grass and herb
>   bound the shifting dunes.
>
> Lastly, men came, led by Christ
> To build a home for restless souls,
> A beacon to shed forth His light.

A traditional prayer of St Aidan for Holy Island reflects the quality of this home of Christ:

> Here be the peace of those who do your will;
> Here be the peace of brother serving other;

Here be the peace of holy monks obeying:
Here be the peace of praise by night and day.

A holy place evokes an atmosphere of devotion. It invites prayer. It carries a story. It can be a means of mission. It inspires encounters with God. It is never enough, though, to honour only those places made holy by past obedience to God. As Jesus told the Samaritan woman, it is not a question of whether this mountain or that holy city is most hallowed: God is Spirit and must be worshipped sincerely wherever we are (John 4:20–4). It is, however, a question of allowing God to lead us to the place he has for us, both in life and in terrain.

Father Brian, Prior of the Monastery of the Saviour, Hove, a few years ago wrote these most helpful words to me:

To wait, to ask, and try to recognise how God, not we, takes the initiative, and makes his love felt amongst us, in places chosen by himself. Just as he chose Galilee to launch his evangelisation (Matthew 4:12–17) and also called people into such places. Once called, these people immediately recognise his choice for them and their hearts are in that place for the rest of their lives. Light has dawned, and nothing will put them off, because the governance of God is at hand.

A Prayer
Lord, make your home in the place you lead me to;
Take that place and fill it with your love:
Make me at home in whatever place you lead me to;
May it reflect a glory all your own.

A Response
I will not rest until I can rest in the place you have for me, and it becomes a place of resurrection.

7

Hospitality

'Remember to welcome strangers in your homes' (Hebrews 13:2).

Hospitality is a Christian virtue in which the Celts excelled. Yet how can it be practised in overcrowded areas in which it is habitually abused?

Hospitality is not only a custom in a home, but a key into the Kingdom of God. It is a matter of honour in the Old Testament (cf. Genesis 19:8; Judges 19:23), and in the early Christian Church (e.g. Titus 1:8). In the New Testament, the Church is described as the household, or home, of God. Every aspect of church life is meant to be an experience of hospitality. So what principles of hospitality can we learn from the Celtic Church?

Hospitality means offering each person we meet a generous heart

Celtic Christians drew inspiration from Desert Fathers and Mothers with regard to hospitality. They learned from Cassian of when he and some friends arrived in Egypt. His friends wondered why the monks they visited had given up their normal practice of fasting. One monk explained: 'Fasting is something I do all the time, but it is my choice. But to love is not a matter of choice. So to offer hospitality to you is to fulfil the law of love; it is to receive Christ.' Another brother visited a solitary hermit, and apologised for making him break his rule of fasting and silence. The solitary replied: 'My rule is to receive you with hospitality and to send you away in peace.'[1]

Hospitality needs to be built around a God-given framework of prayer, work and rest. It means that if I have the time, the energy, the skills and the resources, I will offer these. If I have to refuse, I will open my heart to my supplicant and explain why; I will send him or her on their way with the blessing of a generous spirit.

The Northumbria Community pledge themselves to 'availability'. To be available means that we are willing to give time, shelter or sustenance to anyone, if Christ inspires us. We do not do this upon demand; that would be to become a doormat, and would prevent us being available for God's priorities, but we will be open to it, and we will always have a hospitable heart.

Hospitality means creating a welcoming home

Brigid, the fifth-century Irish saint, was famed for her hospitality. She sang and prayed in the kitchen as she made the butter and the bread that she always had in liberal supply for guests. This prayer has been attributed to her:

> I would prepare a feast and be host to the great High King, with all the company of heaven. The sustenance of pure love be in my house, the roots of repentance in my house. Baskets of love be mine to give, with cups of mercy for all the company. Sweet Jesus, be there with us, with all the company of heaven. May cheerfulness abound in the feast, the feast of the great High King, my host for all eternity.

It was said that Brigid divided her dairy churning into twelve in honour of the apostles, and the thirteenth in honour of Christ; this was reserved for the poor and for guests. That tradition has been maintained in her native Ireland, and is reflected in this Irish grace: 'Bless, O Lord, this food we are about to eat, and if there be any poor creature hungry or thirsty walking along the road, send them into us that we can share the food with them, just as you share your gifts with us all.'[2]

The Northumbria Community suggest that at the family Shabat (weekly shared meal) one extra place is set. This is to welcome the Christ who comes in the guise of the unexpected visitor, and it teaches us to treat with honour whoever may come.

Hospitality means that the local Christian community is 'at home' to people during the week

The monastery that Columba founded at Derry fed 1,000 hungry applicants every day. In Wales, the brothers at David's monasteries would eat bread and water themselves, but cook appetising meals for their guests.

Cuthbert became guest-master at a new monastery at Ripon. One day he found a youth sitting in the guesthouse. Bede tells us 'he got him water to wash his hands, washed his feet himself, dried them, put them in his bosom, and humbly chafed them with his hands'. After Terce, Cuthbert brought him a meal. To Cuthbert's surprise, the youth had gone, though there were no footprints in the snow. When Cuthbert returned the table to the storehouse, he found three heavenly fresh-baked loaves. He was sure God had sent an angel to encourage their ministry of hospitality.

In church, the primary symbol of hospitality is the invitation to all who are hungry to feed on the Living Bread at the Lord's Table. It is a tragedy that this sacrament has for many become a sign of exclusion, though thankfully many reformed churches keep an 'Open Table'. The Table is open to rich or poor, black or white. There are no entrance fees. It has been described as one beggar telling another beggar where they can find food.

Churches should not only have welcome stewards at the door on Sunday, but a welcome throughout the week. A place to sit, to pray; a place where a meal may be shared, where a person may be listened to; displays and facilities where children, old people, businesspeople and deaf people feel they have been identified with.

Hospitality is a sign that a community is alive, that it is not afraid, that it has something valuable to share. To welcome anyone is always a risk; and an over-busy community that opens its doors can become a burned-out community. There is a time for a community, as for an individual, to be alone, to deepen its identity and its intimacy with God; but there is also a time to open wide the doors.

St Patrick's Church in downtown Hove is served by four monks, whose hospitality to wayfarers revealed a need greater than they could meet. Thus the church turned the narthex of its large Victorian building into a night shelter. Wayfarers join with monks and church members for the communal meals at the church.

Hospitality means giving time and encouragement to neighbours

In the seventh century, Caedmon, a herdsman on the farm near Whitby Abbey, felt an outsider. But a fellow worker took the trouble to listen to his dreams, and to take seriously his potential. Abbess Hilda offered him a home, a place where he could be affirmed and cherished. That is hospitality.

It was the same Hilda who offered hospitality of a quite different sort. She offered the leaders of opposing factions a place of friendship, nourishment and prayer in order to try and reconcile their differences.

Hospitality means welcoming all God's creatures

The hospitality of Iona was always one of its greatest features, not only to human beings, but even to birds and beasts. In the time of Columba, a crane – driven off course by fierce winds – was found lying exhausted on the beach. Columba asked a monk to tenderly take the bird to a hut, and to nurse and feed it for three days. After the crane flew off gratefully, Columba said to the monk: 'God bless you, my son, because you have well looked after our pilgrim guest.'[3]

In the delightful legend of Kevin of Glendalough, Kevin was lying on a flagstone with arms outstretched during a Lent vigil. A blackbird began to build a nest in which to lay eggs. Having unwittingly become its host, Kevin maintained this uncomfortable position until the eggs were hatched!

Hospitality means welcoming competitors

It is one thing to offer hospitality to people who show allegiance to your own work, but quite another to welcome people whose allegiance is to someone who may overshadow you. At one time in Wales, Justinian won so many recruits to his Order that his monasteries could not accommodate them. David warmly offered them hospitality in *his* monasteries, which had spare capacity.

Hospitality is a way of life that is due for a comeback. It is the smile that greets friend and stranger. It is the warm embrace, and the welcome of each person as a gift from God, from the new baby in the mother's womb, to the old person nearing their end in a shrivelled frame. Hospitality is the creation of a space in which the other person may feel secure, at ease with himself or herself; it is the encouragement of their gifts and the affirming of their person.

A Celtic rune of hospitality

We saw a stranger yesterday
We put food in the eating place,
    Drink in the drinking place,
    Music in the listening place,
And with the sacred name of the triune God
    He blessed us and our house,
    our cattle and our dear ones.
    As the lark says in her song:
Often, often, often goes the Christ
    In the stranger's guise.

A Prayer

I open my heart to Christ in the stranger,
To Christ in the guise of a colleague in anger
I open my heart to the one who is wounded,
To Christ in the hungry, the lonely, the homeless.

A Response

I will offer a generous heart to all.

8

Real Men, Women and Families

'Jesus grew both in body and in wisdom' (Luke 2:52).

A leader of a city youth network says: 'The main issue for the guys now is identity. Many of them have no male role models. It's not macho to admit the need to talk about how to develop as a person. The result, for many, is despair. There is about one attempted suicide a week.' This is hardly surprising in a culture in which some feminists call for maleness to be abolished.

A young unemployed man started to make items of pottery. While searching for motifs with which to decorate these, he discovered that certain pre-Christian Celtic symbols spoke to his longings for a more human way of life. I asked him why. 'I like the Celtic image of the man. He takes responsibility for his children. And of the woman. The mother nurtures them. There is no sexism. I hate modern society. People think they are above others. Once you think you are above others you destroy family, community and the earth. The Celts knew that we are all of the earth.'

This young man had no inkling that this quality of manhood, of motherhood, and of the family was being spawned in Christian churches. Instead, I suspect, he assumed church-goers reflected the diseased, dysfunctional, judgemental families of society at large.

In a review of Robert Bly's *Iron John: A Book about Men*, Leon J. Poldles writes of his society being

> full of weak men who cannot bring discipline into their own lives or the lives of others, and full, too, of overgrown boys, Peter Pans who want to prolong adolescence to the age of seventy . . . In traditional societies there are often puberty rites in which a boy is taken from his mother by older men and instructed in the mysteries of maleness, rites involving

ritual fights and wounding . . . industrial society broke this pattern . . .[1]

How vital it is to shout from the rooftops that there is a stream within Christianity waiting to be explored by people with longings like that young man, and with needs such as Robert Bly describes.

The male image that Christian converts inherited from their Celtic milieu included the aspects of warrior and hunter; but they also learned gentler expressions of masculinity such as responsibility, outgoing relationships and tough love. The theme of warrior/hero crops up on the graves of pre-Christian Celts in many parts of Europe. Alexander the Great, Caesar and Tacitus all make mention of their fearless battles. Britons have an indelible image of the fierce Queen Boadicea who struck terror into the hearts of her foes, which is immortalised in the chariot memorial opposite the Houses of Parliament. Christianity tempered this fierceness with gentleness – it did not neuter Celtic aggression; it simply redirected it to a higher plane.

The supreme expression of manhood that combines masculine and feminine qualities, the warrior who takes absolute responsibility to combat evil, yet who does this by embracing vulnerability, is Jesus Christ on the cross. In 'The Dream of the Rood', the tree on which Christ was crucified tells its story:

> Then the young warrior
> God the all-wielder
> Put off his raiment,
> Steadfast and strong . . .
> In the sight of many he mounted the cross . . .

The archetype of the environmentally aware 'Green Man' is resurfacing today. Although this image has pre-Christian roots, and has at times taken on some anti-Christian accretions, something in it reflects the true image of God in man. It is not generally realised that this image was only fully developed in the context of sacred Christian art and thought, which eventually gave rise to modern science.[2] However, it can only be realised in Christ the God-Man.

Green Man at its best stands for an irrepressible life that is earthed in the renewing cycle of nature. Green Man has a feeling for the earth and an enjoyment of her produce, the exultant embracing of the needs, functions and senses of the body, and of the responsibilities of mind, body and soul in a spirit of celebration. William Anderson writes:

> The Green Man utters life through his mouth. His words are leaves, the living force of experience. Anciently he was the prophet: now he comes back as the archetype of the Poet . . . renewing the harmony and the unity to the world of nature with inescapable love. The Green Man offers us a new understanding of the relationship between the macrocosm – the universal world – and the microcosm in ourselves. On the macrocosmic scale he symbolised the point at which the creative power in eternity is made manifest in space and time.[3]

New technologies help us to see this elixir in terms of radio, computers, circuits, brain waves, networks of nerve communications, etc.

Man: the workshop of all creatures

The Celtic Christians, like Martin of Tours, uprooted the pagan worship of trees, yet they did not, as did the Puritans later, sever the link with trees or with the elemental forces. On the fifth-century tomb of St Abbe, the daughter of Hilary, the apostle to the Gauls, is the earliest-known example of a Green Man as a disgorger of vegetation.[4] In early Christian art we find examples of the Green Man linked with the death of Christ 'on the tree' and his resurrection bringing life 'from the tree'. Through Christ, these Christians wrought a transformation in the elemental forces. This is seen most clearly in Patrick's Lent vigil on the mountain, when the great-winged black birds that tormented him were transformed into winged angels. The Celtic missionaries brought the greatest source of natural power on earth under the leadership of Christ.

John Scotus Eriugena called man the workshop of all creatures: he has intellect like an angel, reason like a man, sense like an animal, and life like a plant. Eriugena gave new perspective to the ancient image of the sacred tree by interpreting the Garden of Eden as human nature, in which is planted the Tree of Life. This Tree is the Word of God, and is therefore Christ 'who is the spiritual bread by which angels and saved humanity, whose conversation is in heaven, are fed'.[5] Christ is the elixir through which the fullness of manhood is realised. The *Book of Kells* and a similar *Book of Durrow* are peopled with human as well as with animal heads out of which foliage bursts forth.

It is all too easy, though, to be seduced by the ideal of the Green Man. Neo-pagan models of the Green Man fail to take into account that the promise of fullness becomes the experience of futility. The gap between aspiration and experience is in truth unbridgeable. It becomes a mirage. How many men have embraced eros, only to be destroyed by it? The same danger is inherent in a blind embracing of any of the elemental forces. Jesus Christ, as John Scotus Eriugena so clearly understood, is the only wholly Green Man. He flowed with the elemental forces, but harnessed them always to a greater power and purpose. People said of Christ, 'Even the winds and waves obey him' (Mark 4:41).

It was as a result of passionate devotion to Christ that the Celtic saints became, in effect, 'Green Men' who were not enslaved to the elements. They teach us that even a mutilated body can be inhabited by a manly spirit; that another ingredient of manhood is to take responsibility, to face each decision and to decide appropriately.

St David was a Green Man – strongly physical, eloquent, passionate, considerate – who poured forth energies in counselling, teaching and physical work. Each day he had a cold bath, prayed, often with the intensity of tears, and intensely re-lived the passion of Christ in Holy Communion. David's Welsh monks became known as 'the Watermen', partly because they ate no meat, fed on greens and leeks, and drank much water; partly, so it was said, because 'as fish live in water so these men live in God'. They would dig, hoe, saw, cut and draw ploughs yoked to their sweating shoulders, and they would meditate while they worked. The lands around them became fruitful.

This Boat Song, which Columbanus' monks perhaps sang as they rowed up the Rhine against the tide in 610, captures a manhood shorn of romantic frills that was honed in the hard tasks instilled by their Master, Christ:

> The tempests howl, the storms dismay,
> But manly strength can win the day.
> Heave, lads, and let the echoes ring.
>
> For clouds and squalls will soon pass on,
> And victory lie with work well done.
> Heave, lads, and let the echoes ring.

Hold fast! Survive! And all is well,
God sent you worse, He'll calm this swell.
Heave, lads and let the echoes ring.

So Satan acts to tire the brain,
And by temptation souls are slain.
Think lads of Christ, and echo him.

The king of virtues vowed a prize,
For him who wins, for him who tries.
Think lads, of Christ, and echo him.[6]

In David's Welsh monasteries, young men who wished to become monks were kept waiting outside for three days. They had to learn to stand on their own two feet. They had to become men before they tried to make community, or else they would lose touch with their real selves and become parasites. Celtic young men generally not only had the benefit of interaction with an extended family, but in the church they had the opportunity of an *anmchara*, or soul friend. The anmchara was an ordinary flesh and blood person with whom they could explore any aspect of life. Maybe he had a few more years' experience, and he had come through life's tests, but he was certainly not put on a pedestal.

The revival of long-term discipling which is sometimes called 'the cateshumenate' is one way to help create a culture that is conducive to manliness. Each young person is offered a soul friend, and a course of study and action that is tailored to each person's own developmental needs. These may include adventure weekends that combine physical and spiritual activity. In local churches, men and women include spiritually orphaned young people in their own sporting, social and spiritual pursuits.

If the warrior aspect of manhood is meant to convey that the responsibility of the masculine is to discern, confront and shield others from evil without, then the mothering aspect of womanhood is meant to convey that the responsibility of the feminine is to do the same with the evil that is within.

Women

In the society that the Christian Celts inherited, the female principle was important, particularly the maternal nature of the mother. As in many societies, the woman was credited with maintaining the centre, cradling and holding a family together, even when the world outside might be crumbling. Yet unlike other societies, Celtic women were not trapped in male-dominated, belittling stereotypes. Females could be innovators and leaders.

The Celtic Church realised that this was an aspect of their culture that was in accord with the gospel, and they did not need to change it. (If only the Church in the rest of the Empire had seen the need to change its culture's more negative approach to gender, the western Church's negative attitude to women and to sexuality might never have taken such a hold.) The Celtic Church no doubt recalled how their beloved apostle John took Christ's mother Mary into his home at Christ's request, and enabled her to be mother in the Jerusalem household of the early Church. Their women became leaders of communities for men and women.

They accepted the universal church custom that only men could be ordained, but because there was no clericalism, this did not have the effect of marginalising women. When Brigid became a nun in the fifth century, one old bishop was so awe-struck by the aura of holy fire above her that he unintentionally read the words for the consecration of a bishop over her. He told a remonstrating colleague: 'I have no power in this matter; this dignity has been given by God to Brigid.' This, I think, reflects the sense of proportion the Celtic Church kept about ecclesiastical posts in relation to spiritual callings. I suspect this definition I found in a church encyclopaedia might sum up their attitude: 'Maternity is a form of authority derived from nature, while that which is paternal is merely legal'[7].

The Celts placed a high value on both physical and spiritual motherhood. Women in the church, whether married or single, were free to develop new expressions of the maternal instinct in varied careers; and they were liberated enough not to have to deny the 'mother' within. Many a young child who was destined to become a monk or nun was given a Christian foster mother. This fostering combined the practical and the spiritual, and was something single women as well as married women could do.[8]

Brigid has always been a potent symbol of womanhood. She was the spiritual midwife who helped bring Christian Ireland to birth. She became known as 'the Mary of the Gael'. Her father was a pagan chief whom she infuriated by being a mother to the poor, using his goods. Brigid regularly helped her Christian mother (who had been sold to a Druid priest) in the kitchen, where everything she did blossomed. This is reflected in a song she used to sing: 'Mary's Son, my friend, come to bless this kitchen. May we have fulness through you'.[9]

As Abbess of Kildare, Brigid ruled over a monastery of men as well as women, as did later women such as Ebba and Hilda. We learn that Brigid selected the bishop who would perform the sacerdotal duties 'in the churches that she governed'. Brigid became a symbol of the power of a spiritual mother to bear children into everlasting life.

Some of the Celts' most notable women leaders displayed a wholesome balance of feminine and masculine qualities. Bede tells us that all who knew Hilda, the Abbess of Whitby, 'used to call her mother because of her outstanding devotion and grace'. She combined friendship with organisation to such a degree that she was known and loved as 'mother' far beyond her own locality. Aidan and other leaders maintained a close friendship with her, and Bede tells us they 'loved her heartily for her innate wisdom and her devotion to the service of God'. Yet she also taught everyone to 'observe strictly the virtues of justice, devotion, and chastity' and 'compelled those under her direction to devote so much time to the study of the holy Scriptures and to the performance of good works, that there might be no difficulty in finding many there who were fitted for holy orders'.

Families

Sociologists have defined the family of the 1990s as 'an arrangement of beds around a microwave oven and a fridge'. The theory today is that if my spouse does not bring me the instant happiness I crave, then I find another partner who will.

This modern western sickness is in part caused by the flight from the primal; the divorcing of men, women and families from the natural rhythm of life, and the forcing of them into fake autonomy and 'isms'. The psychiatrist Carl Jung observed that self-styled 'progressive' westerners, who thought they had left behind 'primitive' ways, had in fact repressed certain universal primal instincts, such as motherhood. He dreaded the nemesis that this would bring.[10]

In the Bible, the family line is itself a waymark. Why? It gave shape and identity to each individual. Something was handed down: this contained elements of both character and calling. The individual's destiny was linked to it; but in our society the nemesis that Carl Jung dreaded is now upon us.

In the Celtic Church, womanhood, manhood and the family were valued and lived out to the full. The Celts did not, like our society, oppress women, repress femininity, or emasculate men. Women and men had different roles, but equal status. Sex, like everything else in the physical world, was positively embraced as something God-given. Although a calling to the single life was valued, family life was woven into the heart of the Church and society. Homesteads and extended families were part and parcel of the typical monastic settlements – in Ireland especially.

Before Brendan made the momentous decision to sail away to an unknown destination, he gathered his large extended family together for a six-week family consultation with God. He only decided to go ahead when everyone agreed that this venture was of God. Many fruitful years later, at the ripe old age of ninety-three, Brendan died in the arms of his sister.

Marriage was held in high regard in Celtic society, not just in name, but the real thing. Yet the real thing had to be fought for, with every available spiritual resource, as the following story illustrates. An island ferryman, Lugne Tudida, was deformed, and had become physically repugnant to his wife, who refused to have sexual intercourse with him. Lugne felt so deeply that this was wrong that he intercepted Columba on one of his journeys, and asked him to use his authority to change his wife's mind. Columba reminded the wife that she had become 'one flesh' in marriage. Her response was: 'I am willing to do any practical jobs for him, or to separate and go anywhere, even to become a nun, but I will not sleep with that man.' Columba responded: 'You can't go away, because God has joined you together, so I make a proposal: that each of us separately spend a whole day and a whole night in fasting and prayer about this matter.' All three agreed, and the following day a radiant woman informed Columba: 'Overnight my heart has been changed in some unknown way, and the man I hated yesterday I love today.'[11]

Alexander Carmichael captures how this fullness of manhood, motherhood and family was kept alive in the western coasts and isles of Scotland in a celebration called the *Oda*, the last of which was held in 1866. This event was as follows. Before St Michael's Eve, the women and girls pull up the carrots from the fields, the women bake through the night, while the men take each other's horses. On St Michael's Day, the eldest daughter bakes a *struan*, and the young men bring flags from the moorlands. Little struans are made for each member of the family, even for those who have died.

After a meal, and distributing gifts to the poor, the whole family circles the cemetery on horses: husband and wife on one horse, brother and sister on another. Everyone kneels in prayer round the little prayer house. Then they go to the *Oda*, the place where the men compete in athletics and male and female of all ages compete in horse races. They ride without saddle, without shoes. There is circuiting, the old teaching the young the customs of old times; young men and their girlfriends ride away into the machair. Everyone goes to a ball in a large house, contributes food, joins in singing, or brings musical instruments. The young men and women exchange simple gifts in token of good feeling.[12]

Singles

The Celts also valued singleness highly. Single people were affirmed people, because of the extended family networks. I suspect there was little homosexuality. Dr Elizabeth Moberly and others present the evidence that deficit of love from the parent of the same sex is a major cause of homosexuality. This deficit is much more apparent in today's small, pressurised nuclear families than it would be in extended families that provided an abundance of affirming fathers and mothers.

It was considered possible and normal to be a whole person and to be celibate – Jesus Christ was. Sex was considered to be good, but not indispensable. Clergy could be married (Patrick's deacon father and presbyter grandfather were), but celibacy soon became the norm. Many married Christians abstained from sexual intercourse on Saturdays and Sundays, which were set apart for the Lord exclusively.

Sexuality

The western Church's attitudes towards sexuality over the centuries have been distorted, and this has affected attitudes towards God. Celtic Christians would not, I think, get sidetracked into debates as to whether God is a Father or a Mother: God is God.

Nor would they get sidetracked into debates as to whether sex is good or bad. The Fall, to them, was less about sexuality than about disobedience. When God is in the centre, sex becomes sacred. The young, fresh intimacy of Adam and Eve is recovered, and there is not the banal messiness of quick satisfaction. The meaning of sex is the deep desire for intimacy, connection and creation; it is interwoven with the desire for connection with God. That is how we learn about love. Once we try to unweave these things, then God, love, and the sacredness of sex are lost.

A Prayer
O Jesu, true Son of Humanity – a sign:
Give me
Courage to be;
Courage to cradle;
Courage to go to the wild places;
Courage to weep;
Courage to be angry;
Courage to enter the most intimate relationships;
Courage to risk friendships;
Courage to listen;
Courage to lose;
Courage to act;
Courage to love.

A Response
I will come out from behind my defences. I will take responsibility for all that God has put within me, the masculine and the feminine, the light and the shade, the energies and the convictions, and I will journey in trust, without fear or favour, God being my helper.

9

A Cherished Creation

'God saw everything he had made, and it was very good'
(Genesis 1:31).

At Pentecost 1992, world Heads of State held an Earth Summit
at Rio. At the same time, the World Council of Churches hosted
a conference called 'Searching for the New Heavens and the New
Earth'. The delegates at this conference sent an epistle to all the
churches of the world:

> Dear sisters and brothers, we write with a sense of urgency. The
> earth is in peril. Our only home is in plain jeopardy. We are at
> the precipice of self-destruction. For the very first time in the
> history of creation, certain life-support systems of the planet are
> being destroyed by human actions . . . It is extremely urgent that
> we as churches make strong . . . commitments to the emergence
> of new models of society, based in deepest gratitude to God for
> the gift of life and in respect for the whole of God's creation.

Sadly, the model that the western Church came to adopt
is deeply flawed. It has split religion from science, privatised
religion, and used science to violate the earth. Slowly, though,
we are waking up to the fact that there has been a drifting off
course in the western Church under the pressures of Greek
philosophy on the one hand, and secular humanism on the
other hand.

The Greek mentality splits life into compartments. The physical
world of flesh and matter is written off as evil; the material world
is separated from the spiritual. The Roman Church fell into this
way of thinking through some of the ideas of Augustine (354–430).
Augustine was a great man; however, he was nearly destroyed by
the lusts of the flesh, and his conversion, as described in his book

Confessions (written in the year 400), is a tribute to the power of Christ to change a person. But unfortunately, Augustine fell into the trap of condemning not just the lusts of the flesh, but the flesh itself. For Augustine, the fallen world of created matter cannot be redeemed, because its very nature is sinful.

This split thinking is betrayed in Augustine's attitude towards sex. St Paul had suggested that, if Christ was about to return, celibacy might be better than marriage in the sense that it enabled people to be more available for Christ's service,[1] but people like Augustine were saying that celibacy was superior because sex was not good or spiritual. Such people overlooked the significance of Christ's incarnation; for if the Son of God had taken human flesh, then surely the flesh is to be honoured, not rejected.

The Reformed Churches continued this negative attitude towards creation and the atonement. The holiness tradition in Protestantism tends to equate the world with worldliness; nature is squeezed out between the opposing forces of God and the devil. Theologians have often interpreted the Bible through spectacles coloured by these assumptions. They interpret Genesis 1:28 ('have dominion over every living thing') as if it means *domination*. They fail to understand that dominion should be understood as the dominion of a King of Israel, who 'is one who bears and mediates blessings for the realm entrusted to him'.[2]

This outlook has had far-reaching consequences that were not foreseen. It led to a split between religion and science; and it led to secularisation. Secular ideas pander to the illusion that individuals, companies and countries are autonomous; that they should, and can, do whatever brings them short-term profit without taking responsibility for the resulting chain reaction in nature and in society.

It has led to ecological destruction. If flesh and matter are considered as rubbish, then in time that is exactly how they will be treated. Who cares what happens to the stuff you put in the dustbin? The modern world is reaping the awful harvest of this outlook. Oceans and the air zone are treated as rubbish bins. Animal species and forests are being discarded. Capitalism, like communism, shares in common with Puritanism the conviction that the earth is godless.

This flawed theology of creation has brought about a reaction that blames Christianity for our ecological crisis, and that even writes it off. The American historian Lynn White, for example, claims that 'Christianity . . . has made it possible to exploit nature in a mood of indifference to the feelings of natural objects . . . We shall continue to have a worsening ecologic crisis until we reject the Christian axiom that nature has no reason for existence save to serve man.'[3]

The twin idols of size and speed are destroying our planet. The lust for expansion (as distinct from growth, which is organic) compels societies to select and produce from nature's infinite variety only that which satisfies its immediate cravings. All other forms of life are eliminated. Time itself is under attack. The 'time is money' mentality interferes with the natural processes of nature and takes 'the being' out of life.

This theology that fails to cherish the earth has also created a vacuum, which is today being filled with New Age ideas. Now that a world-view that splits off the material from the spiritual is seen to be false, pantheistic views that reject such a split have become widely attractive. Yet New Age or creationist spiritualities are, I believe, equally alien to the authentic Christian birthright, for they fail to address the root of the ecological problem. This lies in universal human nature, not merely in the mind-set of one period of time or tradition. By confusing creation with the Creator they could lead us into a new Dark Age. They 'run the equal danger of worshipping the creation as Creator'.[4]

Where, then, may we look within Christianity for a model such as the World Council of Churches pleads for, a spirituality that celebrates and cherishes the earth? Fortunately, the Church in the east, and the Celtic Church in Britain, offered a better way of looking at creation than did the Roman Church.

In Celtic churches, writes Esther de Waal, 'Christ is celebrated, the centre of the universe, the keystone in the structure which God designed. It is as though the entire universe is simply one whole in which past and present, earth and heaven are embraced. There is no division into two realms, the natural and the supernatural, but the two flow together into one.'[5] That is why in the sixth century Columbanus taught his disciples: 'Understand, if you want to know the Creator, created things'.

In its attitude towards creation, the Celtic Church was reflecting Christianity's Jewish roots. The Jewish tradition sees God as the Moral Creator, the Source and Judge of all. When we violate the laws of morality, we violate the very nature of God, with which the universe is stamped. Jewish commentaries upon Genesis, unlike Christian commentaries, tend not to interpret it as a justification for using the earth other than in a context of relationship to it.

Celtic spirituality sees God reflected in all things. In the plaitwork patterns that are typical in Celtic art, there are no loose ends. These symbolise the continuity of the Spirit through all life. The continual background note or drone maintained behind the music of the bagpipes expresses the same idea. This evokes a communion between all things, which is impossible if God *is* all things.

'If the British Church had survived', wrote H. J. Massingham, 'it is possible that the fissure between Christianity and nature, widening through the centuries, would not have cracked the unity of Western man's attitude to the universe.'[6] What elements in that unifying attitude towards the universe can most contribute to a Christian theology of creation that is adequate to today's global village?

1 *The Celtic Christians looked upon creation as lovable and enjoyable, as did God when he created it (Genesis 1:31).* The following lines, attributed to Columba, portray a love of creation in relation to God: 'Delightful would it be to me . . . to be on the pinnacle of a rock, that I might often see the face of the ocean; that I might see its heaving waves over the wide ocean, when they chant music to their Father . . .'[7]

Dafydd Ap Gwilym, a fourteenth-century Welsh poet, eulogises the thrush:

> What artist could possibly be sweeter than his soft whistling? At matins he reads three lessons to us all, wearing his feathered vestments. Far away across the lands his clear voice is heard as he cries out in the bushes. Prophet of the hillsides, stout author of man's longing, bright poet laureate of woodland song, each splendid note he sings with his sweet vigour in the aisle of a little brook, each lovely verse in passion's metre, each branch of music's art, each song, each gentle knot he ties to please a girl who argues over what is best in love. A preacher, a reader of lessons; sweet, clear and pure is his muse . . .[8]

This enjoyment of God, together with his creatures, has never been quite extinguished in the Celtic lands. Catherine Maclennan told Alexander Carmichael how her mother would get her children to sing a morning song to God as Mary's lark was singing it up in the clouds and as Christ's mavis was singing it yonder in the tree, giving glory to the God of the creatures for the repose of the night, for the light of the day, and for the joy of life.

She would tell us that every creature on the earth here below and in the ocean beneath and in the air above was giving glory to the great God of the creatures and the worlds, of the virtues and the blessings, and would *we* be dumb![9]

In his poem in Welsh, 'The Christ of Nature', the modern Welsh poet Donald Evans captures the way he, doubtless like many Celtic Christians, understood Christ's view of the natural world:

He loved the character of birds, the flock that trusted in His Father; He loved lambs, the most skilfully made: lambs with the most innocent nature. He loved the beasts of the margin-lands; those that dwelt in the wild; He loved their staunch dependence on that which the desert could give. He loved the wheat swaying, weighed down with yellow nourishment; He loved the mountain fastnesses, the uninhabited places where peace grew. He loved the earth; loved her like a relative because she is God's earth; He loved her because she was created by His Father out of nothing as a temple of life.[10]

Of course, this kind of poetic vision is open to the charge of romanticism, of the kind that became prominent in the period in the nineteenth century now known as 'the Celtic twilight'. There was nothing romantic, however, about the hard daily existence of some of the Celtic hermits; and this sense of wonder, though it has been overlaid in our society, is being freshly evoked today in ways as varied as encounters with dolphins and views from space.

Something of the innate wonder evoked by meeting creatures in the wild, and of the desecration of treating them solely as market commodities, is captured by Heathcote Williams in his account of his meetings with dolphins:

Your mind feels re-charged by the nameless wildness of this creature . . .
your mind reaching out and becoming one with another . . .
Its life is lived out in places where a luminous beauty is its daily diet . . .
Raw beauty is a daily rule of life,
Rather than an elitist exception
Tussled over by investors in art

Who crudely see beauty as the hardest currency there is –
The lifeless prop of nest-building pride . . .[11]

For ancient humans, a forest was big enough for them to feel
mortal; but that feeling can easily be lost in today's global village.
Yet access to outer space has something of the same effect, as
Archibald Macleish's words convey: 'To see the earth as it truly
is, small and blue and beautiful, the earth in that eternal silence
where it floats, is to see ourselves as riders on the earth together,
brothers on that bright loveliness in the eternal cold – brothers
who now know that they are truly brothers.' Our destiny is to
have access to the vast universe, something that will never end.
This predisposes us to a relationship with God.

2 *The Celtic Christians saw Christ as the means of restoring
with the created world a communion that had become fragmented.*
They did not deceive themselves that all was well with the world,
or that harmony with it was possible merely 'in the natural'. It
was only through their communion with Christ, the Source and
the Saviour of creation, that communion between themselves and
other creatures was fostered. The Logos, from whom emanated
the energies that resulted in created things, was the Christ of the
cradle, the cross and the crown.

A catechism attributed to Ninian expresses the unity that the
Celtic Church sustained between the Christ of revelation and the
Christ reflected in creation:

What is best in this world? *To do the will of our Maker.*
What is his will? *That we should live according to the laws of
his creation.*
How do we know those laws? *By study – studying the Scriptures
with devotion.*
What tool has our Maker provided for this study? *The intellect
which can probe everything.*
And what is the fruit of study? *To perceive the eternal Word of
God reflected in every plant and insect, every bird and animal,
and every man and woman.*[12]

The Celts' greatest European theologian, John Scotus Eriugena,
wrote in his famed *Homily on the Prologue to the Gospel of St John*:

Consider the infinite, multiple power of the seed – how many
grasses, fruits, and animals are contained in each kind of seed;
and how there surges forth from each a beautiful, innumerable

multiplicity of forms. Contemplate with your inner eye how in a master the many laws of an art or science are one; how they live in the spirit that disposes them. Contemplate how an infinite number of lines may subsist in a single point, and other similar examples drawn from nature. From the contemplation of such as these . . . you will . . . see how all things made by the Word live in the Word and are life.[13]

This sense of Christ's presence in all things is reflected in prayers collected by Alexander Carmichael, such as the following one:

> There is no plant in the ground
> But is full of his virtue,
> There is no form in the strand
> But is full of His blessing . . .
> There is no bird on the wing,
> There is no star in the sky,
> There is nothing beneath the sun,
> But proclaims His goodness.
> Jesu! Jesu! Jesu!
> Jesu! meet it were to praise Him.[14]

3 *The Celtic Christians believed that creation was yet to be transformed into its fullness of divine glory*. The Celtic Christians' close fellowship with God and nature swept away the barrier between them and the animals, and gave them a love for them. In them, Isaiah's vision began to be fulfilled: 'Wolves and sheep will live together in peace, and leopards will lie down with young goats. Calves and lion cubs will feed together, and little children will take care of them' (Isaiah 11:6,7). Legends abound, both humorous and touching, of the part that animals played in God's leading of the Celtic saints.

St Kentigern (AD *c* 518–603), who was known as Mungo, knew God was calling him to found a Christian community among the pagan people of Scotland, but where? A wild hound appeared, and Mungo followed him across mountains and valleys. They slept together at nights. Eventually they came to a river in a valley that was inhabited. Was this the place where God wanted Mungo to found the community? He knelt on the ground and asked God to guide him. It was then that a robin alighted on Mungo's shoulder, flapped its wings, and tweaked his neck. Mungo took this welcome as God's sign that he should build there.

Brynach, the hermit who settled in Pembrokeshire in the sixth century, had a reputation for turning wild beasts into friends. Whenever he moved his hermitage to a new location he would harness his furniture to the two wild stags who were regular visitors (and also excellent furniture removers)! Brynach also had a particularly productive cow. He trained a wolf to send the cow to its pastures each morning, and to send it back again at night.

In his introduction to Ron Ferguson's account of the Iona Community entitled *Chasing the Wild Goose*, the late George MacLeod asks:

> What is the matter? That is the question that the western world is everywhere asking, both in the Church – with its lessening of numbers in all denominations – and in the world, with its ever more ominous nuclear confrontation. The short answer is that 'Matter is the matter.'. . . the Church decided to concentrate on the spiritual and leave the week-day to science . . . The opening chapter of John's Gospel reads 'The world was made by Christ and without Him was not anything made that was made . . .' This means that Christ was and is CREATOR and not just Redeemer.[15]

The book tells how members of the Iona Community seek to restore the wholeness of creation, in the most practical ways, in some of the worst inner-city slums in Scotland.

One modern theologian who calls for a revaluation of previously accepted values in relation to creation is Jürgen Moltmann. He points out that from the beginning creation was lovable and enjoyable, but lacking much, and open to God's future working. Creation is 'available' for disaster and redemption; it is an open process. Redemption is not something separate from creation. God's creative activity is seen equally in creation at the beginning, in the creation of human and saving history, and in the creation of a new heaven and earth. The biblical prophets used the word *barar* more often for new acts of creation by God than for the original creation. God liberates his people from slavery, but he is also, through them, liberating creation from slavery. Closed systems condemn themselves to death. Sin is a closed system. Christ's resurrection is a call to life. Through the resurrection, God calls into existence things that did not exist (Romans 4: 18).[16]

Some of the sciences, such as physics, also help us to revise our way of looking at organisms. Science, we find, is now focused on the network of relationships between man and nature, on the framework that makes us as living beings dependent parts of nature.[17]

Stewards

The Celtic Christians were good stewards of creation, and the Iona Christians in particular were a model of good stewardship. We can learn from them that to be friends of the earth we must also be friends of God. I have already referred to the story of the exhausted crane swept by the wind on to the beach at Iona. Columba instructed a monk to 'take care to lift it up tenderly, and carry it to some nearby house, where you will diligently feed and care for it three days and nights'.[18]

Columba's Iona monks also took care, when they used up the earth's resources for development, to replenish it and to care for those who made their livelihood from it. They once constructed a hospice made of faggots taken from the field of a peasant named Findchan. Columba learned that the peasant was upset at the loss of the faggots. 'Let us take him twice three pecks of barley,' he said, 'and let him sow at once in his ploughed land.' Findchan was grateful, but since midsummer was past he did not believe he could reap any harvest from them. His wife urged him to sow the seeds, however, since she sensed that God was in this. God had indeed given Columba the insight that Findchan would reap an extra harvest in August. Findchan then worked the land hard, and the second harvest duly came, to the wonder of the whole neighbourhood.

We need to discover again that there is a unity at the heart of our world in Christ, and for this we need humility. A longing is growing in our world for a creation that is not threatened by human beings, but is contemplated. The fate of the planet will be good if it is decided, not in the temples of pressure and panic, but in the quiet places of prayer. An increasing number of people are beginning to follow such a path.

The Way of Life of the new Community of Aidan and Hilda includes a section on Care for and Affirmation of Creation. It states:

> We affirm God's creation as essentially good, but spoilt by the effects of human sin and satanic evil. We therefore respect nature and are committed to seeing it cared for and restored. We aim to be ecologically aware, to pray for God's creation and all his creatures, and to stand against all that would seek to

violate or destroy them. We look upon creation as a sacrament, reflecting the glory of God, and seek to meet God through his creation, to bless it, to celebrate it.[19]

The call to Christians to rediscover the interconnectedness of all things, and to cherish the earth for God, is being heeded even in unlikely places. One busy member of this Community resolves to walk regularly so as consciously to appreciate God's creation. Similarly, a member of a church in an inner-city area rented an allotment, made it a place of beauty, placed in it a simple shed for shelter, and invited his fellow members to use it as a place of refreshment.

A Celtic Eucharist published by the Community of Aidan and Hilda reintroduces us to the concept of Christ as the Bough of Creation. St Paul presents Christ as the first, and therefore the best, of creation (Colossians 1:15); the Celts expanded on this. They understood that the supreme specimen of the divine energies that brought forth the earth and the heavens is Jesus Christ. Thus the Eucharist proclaims: 'Risen Christ, we welcome you. You are the flowering Bough of creation'; and after the bread and wine have been received: 'Heaven is inter-twined with earth. Alleluia!'[20] In the supreme sacrament of Christianity, we see that God takes up the material, changes it, and makes it his own.

A Prayer

When the Saviour of this globe was stretched out on the tree
  of death,
the elements erupted and the earth gave up its dead. His blood,
  spilled on
the soil, transfigured earth and heaven.

May your body and blood change us and transfigure this earth.
Transfigure this earth: may life be renewed on it.
Transfigure this earth: may your kingdom come on it.
Transfigure this earth: may flowers bloom on it.
Transfigure this earth: may all creatures be friends on it.[21]

A Response

I resolve that my eating be a celebration of the goodness of God's earth; that my working be a cherishing of God's creatures great and small; that my resting be a contemplation of the wonder of God's world.

10

The Cross in Creation

'God made peace through his son's death on the cross and so brought back to himself all things, both on earth and in heaven' (Colossians 1:20).

You cannot redeem what you do not understand. The only person who can redeem creation is someone who understands it from the inside. St Paul here clearly teaches that the scope of Christ's saving work on the cross includes not just individuals, but the whole of creation. 'There was a cross in the heart of God before there was one planted outside Jerusalem, and now that the cross of wood has been taken down, the one in the heart of God abides.'[1] Christ the Lamb is also the Beginning and the End (Revelation 22:2,13).

Jesus and Paul saw intimations of the cross in nature: the grain of wheat 'dying' in the winter earth before it could burst into life in spring (John 12:24; 1 Corinthians 15:36). The first Christians, who were not free to make direct representations of such an object of disgust as the cross, used to see it in the flight of a bird, in the shape of a tree or of a human figure. Today, physics throws new light on how the cross is written into the very stuff of matter; the rhythm of death and resurrection occurs throughout the cosmos. But only as we look at the universe through the spectacles of the Creator's 'Sacrifice of Love', do we truly comprehend its meaning. The cosmos has been preserved and strengthened by the cross.

It was Christ who accompanied Moses' people in baptism, cloud and fire centuries before the events at Golgotha (1 Corinthians 10:2–5). Baptism, the pattern of dying and rising that we see in nature and in Christ, remains a pattern we are to follow. One workaholic minister began to understand the need to reflect this pattern in his own life: 'I start spring worn out, yet everything else in nature springs exhuberantly to life. Why the discrepancy? Nature uses winter to gather strength. I use it to dissipate energy in a welter of activities. We should go at winter's pace in winter.'

Similar to the approach of the Creationist writer Matthew Fox, Celtic spirituality believes in original blessing; but, unlike Fox, it recognises that sin is so radical that it attacks the origins as well as the margins of everything. There is nothing that does not need to be redeemed. Andrew Walker has written that the Celts, like the eastern Church, believed that

> the cosmos is enslaved to evil. It is not evil in itself. It is in thrall to demonic powers, and its human representatives have betrayed it. God became man in order to set the cosmos, including us, free from bondage . . . The moment that God entered into material creation he declared it holy in his own body . . . The atonement of God is the at-one-ment with the whole creation in the person of Jesus.[2]

A cross breaking through a circle, carved on a pillar of stone, is the typical Celtic symbol. Pillars of stone were a universal symbol of the link between heaven and earth. The circle round the cross was introduced by the Emperor Constantine as a symbol of the wreath of victory. But only in Celtic lands did it remain fashionable, probably because the circle also came to represent the created world, which the Celts so highly valued. The Celtic cross speaks of victory, wholeness, the transforming power of Christ in all creation.

The old pagan and today's New Age philosophies offer us a circle without a cross. The Augustinian philosophy offered a cross without a circle. Our world stands in need of both the cross and the circle.

If we relate to the creation with the idea that we can abandon ourselves to all that the circle represents, we find ourselves enslaved. Matthew Fox's call, in his influential book *Original Blessing*, to embrace Eros as if Eros is God is an example of this.

Seeing creation through 'washed eyes'

The Celtic saints were able to see creation in its God-intended glory only because their eyes had first been 'washed'. As Robin Flower observes: 'It was not only that these scribes and anchorites lived by

the destiny of their dedication in an environment of wood and sea;
it was because they brought into that environment an eye washed
miraculously clear by continuous spiritual exercise that they, first
in Europe, had that strange vision of natural things in an almost
unnatural purity.'3

> O Son of God, do a miracle for me and change my heart; Thy
> having taken flesh to redeem me was more difficult than to
> transform my wickedness. It is Thou, who, to help me, didst
> go to be scourged by the Jews; Thou dear child of Mary, are
> the refined molten metal of our forge. It is Thou who makest
> the sun bright, together with the ice; it is Thou who createst
> the rivers and the salmon all along the river . . . Though the
> children of Eve ill deserve the birdflocks and the salmon, it
> was the Immortal One on the cross who made both salmon
> and birds.4

The Bible records that at Jesus' crucifixion the sun was hidden
and the earth quaked (Matthew 27: 45, 51). Celtic Christians took
to heart the implications of this. Their poetry gives us the sense that
in the suffering of God, all creation is involved and transformed.
The tree in the garden that brought death has become the tree on
the hill that brings life. Through the senses that God has given us,
we are involved in the joy of life – but we are also vulnerable to its
pain. In 'The Dream of the Rood', the tree on which Christ was
crucified tells its story:

> In the sight of many he mounted the cross . . .
> Those sinners pierced me . . .
> Dark clouds overspread
> The sheen of the heavens,
> The shadows lay heavy
> Pale under heaven
> All creation wept
> The death of its maker.5

The following is a poem called 'The Crucifixion':

> At the cry of the first bird
> They began to crucify Thee,
> O cheek like a swan,
> It were not ever right to cease lamenting – it was like the
> parting of day from night.6

Blathmac, an eighth-century Irish poet, retold the biblical epic in long narrative poems; these were part of a movement that produced the great stone crosses upon which biblical stories were depicted. Of the crucifixion he wrote:

> The sun concealed its proper light; it lamented its lord. A swift cloud went across the blue sky, the great stormy sea roared. The whole world became dark, great trembling came on the earth; at the death of noble Jesus great rocks burst open . . . A fierce stream of blood boiled until the bark of every tree was red . . . It would have been fitting for God's elements – the fair sea, the blue sky, the earth – to have changed their appearance, lamenting their calamity. The body of Christ exposed to the spear'thrust demanded harsh lamentation – that they should have mourned more grievously the Man by whom they were created.[7]

A Prayer
May the CROSS of Christ be between me and the Destroyer;
May the CROSS of Christ be between earth and the Polluter;
May the CROSS of Christ be between galaxies and the Usurper;
May the CROSS of Christ be between after-life and the Deceiver.

A Response
I make my soul and the entire universe an altar; I pray for Christ's redeeming work from within the depths of creation.

11

A World of Sacrament

'Ever since God created the world his invisible qualities, both his eternal power and his divine nature, have been clearly seen; they are perceived in the things that God has made' (Romans 1:20).

Every human being, St Paul tells us, can get clues from the nature of creation as to the nature of the Creator. The sheer size, intelligence and variety of creation speak of an infinite mind and energy. The beauty and detail of every stone, petal or fingerprint point to the wonder of the Almighty. Jesus, like Paul in his letter to the Romans, knew that every thing in creation bears witness to its Creator. 'Even if my supporters were to keep quiet', he told the critics who complained about their noisy acclaim as he rode into Jerusalem on a donkey, 'the stones themselves will start shouting' (Luke 19:40). Jesus, Paul, and countless Jews and Christians since, loved to repeat words from the psalms such as, 'The heavens declare the glory of God' (Psalm 19:1).

Yet the vision of God is vanishing from the earth: that is the conclusion of some of today's most significant thinkers. An example of this blindness to the obvious is a BBC Radio 4 interview between church leader Gerald Coates and an atheist professor of mathematics. The professor chided Coates: 'Gerald Coates believes God creates something out of nothing! It is so irrational, how can you get your mind around that?' Coates responded: 'I confess that God creating something out of nothing is a difficult concept to get your mind around. But what does the Professor believe? That nothing – created something – out of nothing! That is a lot more difficult to get your mind around.'[1]

Much of this loss of the power to see eternal realities reflected in material things is caused by the mind-set of the Enlightenment ('only things that humans can measure are real') allied to technology, which saturates nearly every corner of life with data and images that blanket out that which is eternally real.

A profound service that the Church can offer to today's world is to recapture a sacramental way of looking at the world. Tragically, Protestantism has unwittingly played the Enlightenment's game, and Catholicism has played devil's advocate. Many Protestants reject symbols, ceremonies and a sacramental understanding of the world for two reasons, both of which have some weight. First, because these came to reflect formalism, rather than a living experience of God; they were thus in danger of becoming idolatry. Second, because God communicated through the Word (Christ) and through words (now enshrined in the Bible). Without the precision of words, they argue, the purity of the gospel message is lost; visual means of communication rely upon feelings and imagination, which can easily lead people astray.

Those who take this view are seldom logical. A Protestant who spurns a candle in church on Sunday will celebrate an anniversary at a candlelit restaurant on a Saturday, because he values the atmosphere it can create. People who condemn icons as the worship of images go home to watch unholy images on their television screens, and give their children Bibles that contain holy images, i.e. pictures.

Protestantism needs to be healed of its fear of visual and material things. Selwyn Hughes, the Protestant author of the *Every Day With Jesus* Bible Notes, writes about Moses' experience of God in the burning bush (Exodus 3). While it is true, he says, that people have been led astray by basing their conclusion about God on their subjective experiences rather than on the objectivity of Scripture, Scripture itself includes many instances of God getting people's attention through something they see. He concludes:

We should be alert and ready to discover the revelation of God in the common places of life . . . It is possible to walk about blind to the glory that is around us because we do not expect to find it there. Therefore we need the discerning eye – the power to see the glory in the ordinary, to walk down familiar pathways and see unfamiliar things, and to hear the accents of Jesus in spite of a dialect. This was the thought the poet had in mind when he penned the famous lines:

> *Earth's crammed with heaven*
> *And every bush afire with God.*[2]

Rekindling a Christian imagination

It is true that in the Roman Church the Christian imagination had become too one-tracked. Such an imagination needs to be constantly renewed and re-clothed through fresh experience of God. Nevertheless, the Protestant position was fundamentally unbiblical, because it did not acknowledge the way God has actually chosen to make reality. It separated the spiritual from both the physical and the imaginative aspects of creation.

The eastern and the Celtic churches never fell into this false dualism. Columbanus taught the people of his day: 'If you want to know the Creator, first understand and know creation!' St Patrick taught people to say a creed that reminded them to see God in all things:

> Our God is the God of all people,
> The God of heaven and earth.
> The God of sea, of river, of sun and moon and stars,
> of the lofty mountains and the lowly valleys.
> The God above heaven.
> The God under heaven,
> The God in heaven.
> He has his dwelling round heaven,
> and earth and sea, and all that is in them.
> He inspires all,
> He quickens all,
> He dominates all,
> He sustains all.

This spirituality lives on in today's Iona Community, as Ron Ferguson proclaims: 'Prayer becomes as natural as breathing. The material is shot through with the spiritual; there is a "within-ness" of God in all life. The whole earth is sacramental: everything is truly every blessed thing . . .'[3]

David Adam reminds us that the Celtic Church could

> see in the visible things those things which are invisible more easily than we do today. They were aware of creation pointing towards its Creator, and because creation has a Creator, we are

offered a relationship through it to him . . . Created things spoke to them of the goodness and love of the Creator who was involved in and with his creation. He was not a God who had left it to run itself. So, creation was the means of communion with Father, Son, and Holy Spirit. Everything spoke of a Presence, vibrated with his love. They saw a universe ablaze with His glory, suffused with a presence that calls, nods and beckons – a creation personally united with its Creator in every atom and fibre . . . We need to regain a sense of wonder, reverence and awe.[4]

As we consider our Celtic heritage, what faculties do we need to rekindle?

We must rekindle the faculty of purified imagination. In 1867, the Scottish author George MacDonald attempted to rescue imagination from its prison in contemporary world-denying orthodoxies. He wrote in an essay entitled 'The Imagination, Its Functions and Its Culture' that creation was an exercise of God's imagination, and man embodies the thought of God. Thus 'the imagination of man is made to the image of the imagination of God'.[5] He accepted that imagination, like any other faculty, can become depraved or deprived, but he regarded it as the leader of its brother human faculties in opening up the way forward.

The Irish mystic and theologian Noel Dermot O'Donoghue explores the Celtic way of seeing in his book *The Mountain Behind the Mountain*. The Celts saw *into* nature, discerning shapes and presences that were at once physical and spiritual. Thus there was the eternal sun within the physical sun. O'Donoghue calls this way of seeing *imaginal*. It is not a faculty that projects inner fantasies on to the world; it is a faculty that perceives what is really there, but that is not obvious to people who lack this faculty.[6]

Therefore in order to be imaginal, a person must heed Jesus' statement that it is the pure who shall see God (Matthew 5:8). Brother Aidan, who is a young Orthodox monk and icon painter, clarifies this point:

The imagination is a faculty for seeing, rather than for inventing. Its creativity consists in opening the door from the patently visible to the latently visible. It extends the beam of the spiritual eye through the sensual into the realm of the spiritual. Put another way, the imagination, when properly functioning, registers on the retina of the soul the rays of uncharted light with which the 'bush' of creation is burning without being consumed. As the eye is a sense faculty of the body, so is the healthy imagination a sense organ of the spiritual mind. It can receive spiritual truths from the material world. But *purity of heart* is required for such a healthy functioning of the imagination. Without this purity, the ever active mind and imagination construct disjointed thoughts and representations that bear little resemblance to reality. Such images debase rather than dignify; they vandalise rather than draw people closer to the spiritual *logoi* within creation.[7]

The Celtic way of seeing

Noel Dermot O'Donoghue concludes:

There is a sense in which Europe is the creation of the monks who journied into the darkness with this Celtic way of seeing, for the light that troubled their dreams had to shine *into* the darkness; it was a Christian light, incarnate, sacrificial. It was a light and a vision that had been tested and purified and deepened in the darkness of Gethsemane and Calvary, a light breaking forth from the Cross, an Easter light, a vision of the Risen Lord who was 'the Son of the gentle Mary'.[8]

We begin to see that essential to a spirituality for a new culture is the interweaving of the different threads. Without the desert, the contemplation, we will be without the purity; without purity, there can be no truly Christian imagination.

We must rekindle awareness that the Higher can be transposed to the lower. This century, the Oxford trio of C. S. Lewis, J. R. R. Tolkien and Charles Williams, who were known as the 'inklings', have attempted to rekindle the Christian imagination. Tolkien believed that 'legends and myths are largely made of "truth", and indeed present aspects of it that can only be received in this mode'.[9] He wanted to leave a body of legends for England that others could build upon. He told the sceptical C. S. Lewis, who at one time thought the Gospels were 'only myth', that Lewis suffered from a 'failure of imagination', because he had failed to see that in the unique instance of the

Gospels, the myth of all myths had become incarnated in flesh and blood.

Lewis was later to write about a principle in the universe that he calls transposition, the power of the higher to be incarnate in the lower. In *The Pilgrim's Regress*, he expresses this pictorially: '. . . as people become pagans again, the Landlord again sends them pictures and stirs up sweet desire and so leads them back to Mother Kirk even as he led the actual pagans long ago. There is indeed, no other way.'[10]

This idea of the Logos, of spiritual hierarchies penetrating the world of flesh and blood, was natural to Greek and Druid ways of thinking. Our world needs to recapture the vision of the Unseen Reality that lies behind the everyday realities. It equally needs to recapture Christianity's revelation that, unlike the pagan and New Age teachings, the Higher is most fully disclosed in Jesus Christ, and he is the Lord of the unseen world.

As we saw in an earlier chapter, the Celtic theologian John Scotus Eriugena explained the principle of transposition clearly in his homily on the prologue to John's Gospel, which contains the amazing truth that 'the logos . . . became a human being' (John 1:14). The principle of transposition, in a wider form, was clearly taught in the catechism that tradition attributes to St Ninian. It ends: 'And what is the fruit of study? *To perceive the eternal Word of God reflected in every plant and insect, every bird and animal, and every man and woman.*'

Each month and each season say something to us of God's love. For example, November mist is like one's outer aura, mysterious, sombre, beautiful, a prelude to something clearer and nearer one's heart. In it I may be lost in wonder and prayer.

We must rekindle the place of poetry in our national and church life. Bards played a key part in Celtic life. They were the story-tellers, poets and songsters who, together with the seers who interpreted the meaning, passed on the message so that it 'touched the parts' that the formal functionaries could not reach. This enabled Christianity to survive fierce ideological onslaughts.

Perhaps children will lead the way, for they have not had time to expunge the poetic instinct that God has planted within us. Leonie Caldecott has written:

Children are not stupid enough to think that beauty is second-ary. Given half a chance, they will sacramentalise the minutiae of everyday life with a flower here, a drawing there, a song for every occasion. The soul of a poet is the soul of a child. It is a King David, dancing before the Ark one moment, and next bewailing his own folly, his sins, the loss of the presence of the Holy One. It is the voice of human experience seeking out its God, with praise and entreaty, tears and laughter, murmurings and minuets. A voice stilled at our peril. And chased from our liturgy at our peril.[11]

Poetry has never been stilled in the soul of Wales, as this Welsh poet illustrates: 'The face of nature laughs in the springtime, her breath fresh and her eyes clearest blue . . . The sun glints through the fresh green leaves; the wind rustling through the branches is the harp of nature, playing a song of love. Men are vigorous and strong, women pretty and gay; the whole world is in love with its Creator.'[12]

The value of symbols

We must rekindle the appreciation of symbols. The Swiss psy-chiatrist Carl Jung believed that true transformation of persons happened largely through contact with images, or archetypes. They have the power, which words do not have, to connect a person to an unseen reality. Archetypes generate power, for good or evil. Leanne Payne calls upon Christians to re-create a biblical symbolic system to replace the vacuum created over recent centuries.[13] If we do not do this, the devil will. Why should the devil have all the best symbols? Jesus' ministry overflowed with acted and spoken symbols. The Celtic Church used water and oil, flame and stone, and, in their beautiful illuminated manuscripts, colour, craft and contour.

We must rekindle the faculty of memory. The command 'Remem-ber!' was one of the keys in the spiritual formation of Israel; it makes for a rewarding Bible study. The command 'Do this in memory of me' was one of the keys in Jesus' plan for the future of his new people (Luke 22:17). In the original language, Jesus' words 'This is my body *given for you*' related to past, present and future (*to didomenon*). In Jesus, the past and the future become present. History is treated as irrelevant by many people, especially the English; yet if history is Jesus' story, he can take past experiences that we may think are gone for ever, and make us aware that they still retain their connection with the Source, as we do. It is in Jesus that the past, too, becomes sacramental. This is what T. S. Eliot calls 'the point of intersection of the timeless with time'. At that point, events that have passed away are rediscovered and generate a fresh significance and energy.

This understanding was second nature to the Celts, and the Irish still retain the tradition of 'keening' in poetry and song. A lost world is found by being looked at in the eternal light of memory. Alexander Carmichael includes many examples of this, in the form of yearly rituals, most notably the Easter Sunrise gathering: 'The people say that the sun dances on this day in joy for a risen Saviour. Old Barbara Macphie saw "the glorious gold-bright sun changing colour – green, purple, blood-red, white, intense white, and gold-white, like the glory of the God of the elements to the children of men. It was dancing up and down in exaltation at the joyous resurrection of the beloved Saviour of victory".'[14] The Celts had a vivid belief in a life beyond death.

We must rekindle our awareness of the world as a sacrament. 'The nature of the world is sacramental. It is real and concrete in itself,' writes Andrew Walker, 'but it signifies its otherness and origin outside itself.'

Jesus saw a mustard seed, Paul saw a grain of wheat – these things contain an analogy with the eternal. They have their own function in their own terms, but they also include the image of the invisible world.

The interpretation of the world as a theophany (an expression of the presence of God) finds its true realisation only in Christianity; without Christ, it becomes idolatry. The Good – and Beautiful – is Christ. If objects give us an inkling of God, then drawing near to God give objects their true meaning. If we are not close to God, we appropriate and take over nature. In Christ we cherish wisdom: 'It is he who gave me unerring knowledge of what exists, to know the structure of the world and the activity of the elements: the beginning and the end of middle times, the alternation of the solstices, and the changes of the seasons, the cycles of the year and the constellations of the stars, the natures of the animals and the tempers of wild beasts, the powers of spirits and the reasonings of men, the varieties of plants and the virtues of roots . . .' (Wisdom 7:17–21).

A sacramental approach to life does not directly save souls; but it does predispose people to think about God. 'As the rain hides the stars, as the autumn mist hides the hills, happenings of my lot hide the shining of thy face from me. Yet if I may hold thy hand in the darkness it is enough. Since I know that, though I may stumble in my going, Thou dost not fall.'[15]

A Prayer

I WELCOME the created light of this new day so that I may enter more fully into the uncreated light of eternity;

I WELCOME the wind that blows away all that is not rooted, so that I may enter unencumbered, into the Source of all;

I WELCOME the dark storm clouds so that I may never make light of the mysterious Presence;

I WELCOME the cold so that I may always search for the warming fire of God's love.

A Response

I will look for God's presence in all creation, and will never treat it as an inert commodity.

12

The Eternal Struggle

'For we are not fighting against human beings, but against the wicked spiritual forces' (Ephesians 6:12).

Some Christians regard spiritual warfare as an indispensable key to the advance of Christianity; others think of it as the worst kind of male chauvinist religion, and have campaigned to be rid of it. To them, it speaks of destruction, negativity, scapegoating – and of breeding enemies. It is rare for the two sides to get beyond the stereotyping and to hear one another's viewpoints.

St Paul uses alternatives to military metaphors – such as wrestling; racing; light and darkness; good and bad fruit. Also, the word 'war' itself may be thought of in terms of a mercy rescue mission. Can our Celtic mentors throw further light on this subject? Five separate episodes in the life of Cuthbert illumine different aspects of this issue:

1 *The struggle against fickle ways*. Cuthbert and his colleagues were thrown out of Ripon Monastery, and all that they had laboured to build up was handed over to worldly monks. Bede observed: 'The ways of this world are as fickle and unstable as a sudden storm at sea . . . Yet this change did not weaken our athlete of Christ in his determination to do battle for Heaven.'[1] For Cuthbert, spiritual warfare meant steely determination to reflect the life of heaven, and the absence, not the presence, of retaliation. This determination was to continue even if, in the world's terms, he had 'lost'.

2 *The struggle against merciless elements*. Some time after this, Cuthbert and two colleagues were marooned on a remote coast, cut off by a violent storm and dying of hunger and cold. 'Let us storm Heaven with prayers,' urged Cuthbert, 'asking that same

Lord who parted the Red Sea and fed his people in the desert to take pity on us in our peril. I believe that, unless our faith falters, he will not let us go fasting on this day of Epiphany. Let us look for the banquet he will surely provide for us to keep his festival with joy.' After this they found three cuts of dolphin meat ready to cook, prepared by human hands, and three days later were able to sail home.[2] For Cuthbert, spiritual warfare meant using intercession to change circumstances that obstruct God's good purposes. No enemies were involved.

3 *The struggle against demonic group dynamics*. Cuthbert was preaching to a great crowd when he sensed that he must forestall a plot that the devil was hatching in order to disperse his hearers. 'Listen with complete attention and don't let the devil distract you from hearing what concerns your eternal salvation, for he has a thousand crafty ways of harming you,' Cuthbert warned the crowd. Soon, sheets of flame swept through the whole village and the crowd rushed madly, throwing water on the flames. This was to no avail since it was a phantom fire. However, because Cuthbert had warned them of this, they shamefacedly came to their senses and Cuthbert was able to carry on his exhortations. People in the crowd now said they knew that the 'devil 'did not cease for even an hour in his warfare against man's salvation'. The experience of the build-up of corporate dynamics that destroy what is good is real enough, as was seen this century in Nazi Germany. For Cuthbert, spiritual warfare meant leadership that was so in touch with God that he was one step ahead.

4 *The struggle to deliver individuals from oppression*. A dear friend of Cuthbert, Hildmer, the king's sheriff, and his wife were both devout Christians, yet on one occasion she was seized with terrible convulsions, that involved her letting out frightful howls and gnashing her teeth. The sheriff rushed to ask for Cuthbert's ministry, but shrank from telling him that it was no ordinary illness, fearing that if Cuthbert found she was mad he might think that she did not have a true faith. Cuthbert told his weeping friend, 'Although you are ashamed to tell me, I know that she is afflicted by a demon and that the demon will have left her before we meet her. It is not only the wicked who are stricken down in this way. God, in his inscrutable wisdom, sometimes lets the innocent be blighted by the devil in mind as well as in body.' The woman was totally restored. For Cuthbert, demons were real, but he would never impute blame, or let a person be diminished or trapped

because of a demon, since the love of God was his driving force, over which the demons had no ultimate hold.

Although the Celtic Christians knew that the world of the spirit penetrates the physical world at every point, they also knew that there is good and evil in the spirit world as well as in the human world, and that there is a battle to be fought in both. They were well equipped to fight it.

5 *The struggle to clean out devils' strongholds for God*. The heroes of those early Christians were the people who went into the 'front-line' to confront the powers of evil in places remote from everyday affairs, sometimes after many years of busy work for God. Bede tells us that Cuthbert sought out 'a remote battlefield', the Inner Farne Island. 'The island was haunted by devils; Cuthbert was the first man brave enough to live there alone. At the entry of our soldier of Christ armed with "the helmet of salvation, the shield of faith and the sword of the Spirit which is the word of God", the devil fled and his hosts of allies with him.'[3]

Columba, whose Rule Cuthbert followed, had breathtaking experiences of spiritual warfare. During a day of prayer, alone in Iona, a host of black demons fought against him with fiery darts. The Holy Spirit revealed to him that these demons wished to destroy the monastery and many of the brothers. Adamnan tells us that he 'single-handed, against innumerable foes of such a nature, fought with the utmost bravery, having received the armour of the apostle Paul'. The contest was maintained for the greater part of the day. The demons could not vanquish Columba, nor could he vanquish them, until angels came to his aid and the demons fled to another island, whose monastery succumbed to the plague. This story echoes that of Jesus and the Gadarene swine.[4]

Natural and spiritual processes

In recent centuries we have learned more about physical, social and psychological processes. Thoughtful Christians repudiate those immature methods used by Christians that show no understanding of these processes, or which divorce spiritual warfare from social care. Some theologians, such as Lesslie Newbigin in his *The Gospel in a Pluralist Society*, include amongst the biblical 'powers and principalities' human institutions that accrue a group dynamic greater than the individuals within the institution.[5] The tenor of Cuthbert's life suggests that, had he lived today, he would have disputed none of these things. What Cuthbert grasped, which Christians with an Enlightenment mind-set lost sight of, was that spiritual processes are at the pinnacle of all processes.

A dismissive view of the reality of good and evil powers in the supernatural as well as in the natural sphere led to cynicism and powerlessness in the Church, and to a vacuum in the soul of the people. It is being filled today with a glut of films, books and groups that glorify the occult, the elements or the erotic. Cuthbert's example calls women and men today to become athletes in the eternal arena. There is no situation in peace or war that cannot be turned around through unrelenting intercessory prayer. Christians must replace no-go areas for God with the Kingdom of God.

There were occasions when this kind of spiritual warfare changed the outcome of a military battle, as in the famous victory of King Oswald against a vastly superior and godless invader in A.D. 634 Oswald planted a cross in the ground and knelt in prayer with his small army to invoke heavenly aid, 'for He knows we are fighting in a just cause for the preservation of our whole race'. Ever since, that place has been known as 'Heaven field'; it reminds us that there is no field of human endeavour that cannot be touched by God through prayer.

Some feminists regard everything to do with spiritual warfare as male, and they think maleness is always about domination; thus it should not be part of a spirituality designed for the twenty-first century. If it is true that 'the warrior' is an inherently male archetype, the work of the Holy Spirit is to redeem 'the warrior' so that it becomes power for good, life and creativity.[6] A spirituality that is adequate for the needs of the coming millennium must give full worth to masculine and to feminine, both of which reside in women and men.

The gentle Aidan, who was in touch with his feminine as much as with his masculine, engaged in the eternal struggle when he lay on the good earth of the Inner Farne in prayer. He saw the ferocious invader Penda piling Bamburgh with flammable material that was about to destroy it in a conflagration. As he prayed, the wind turned, the fire subsided, and Penda retreated.

The enterprising Brigid, who was in touch with her masculine as much as with her feminine, engaged in spiritual warfare when she visited a place where her nuns feared to preach God's word because of a madman. Brigid directly confronted the man, and challenged him to preach God's word himself, which he did!

The earliest Celtic evangelists had to confront evil of a different kind: false teachings that destroyed or distorted goodness as revealed in Christ. St Kentigern (also known as Mungo) re-established Christianity in the north-west by proclaiming as false the elemental forces that the people worshipped as gods. At a time when drought and pests had decimated the crops, he took the initiative in the name of God. The elemental forces were the creations of God, provided to help people, he explained. He called on God to lift the curse on the land, and he called on the people to renounce their worship of what God had created and to worship only the Creator himself. Green shoots sprang from the barren earth and many people turned to God.

Earlier, in Ireland, Brigid had also taken the offensive against worship of the elements. She called God 'the Lord of the elements', and in the name of the Triune God she called forth fertility and blessing in crops and dairy. People actually witnessed that better results came from living God's way than from manipulating the personified forces of nature.

Putting the world right

Patrick was the first to model this way of turning the tables on nature worship. He loved and cherished creation as much as anyone; but he confronted the Druidic religion in the most daring and dashing way, with momentous consequences. At the Druid stronghold at Tara, he lit a fire to mark Christ's resurrection, a better and stronger power than all the magic of the shamans. His prayers were mighty, and the 'St Patrick's Breastplate', a version of which is in many hymnbooks, surely captures something of their spirit:

This day I call to me . . . God's shield to protect me . . . from snares of the demons, from evil enticements, from failings of nature . . . from dark powers that assail me . . . against knowledge unlawful that injures the body, that injures the spirit . . . for my shield this day I call a mighty power, the Holy Trinity'

The 'New Age' world-view today requires a similar challenge from Christ's people. Like Druidism, it is pervasive; there is much that is right about it as well as much that is wrong, but it ultimately leads to a new slavery. 'New Age' is an umbrella term for a range of ideas and practices, but I believe that, at heart, it can be described as 'modern nature worship'.

As popularised by film stars such as Shirley Maclaine, the New Agers claim that we are leaving the Age of Pisces, which is characterised by the imposition of divisive norms (e.g. dogmas and morals), particularly from the Judeo-Christian tradition, and we are entering the Age of Aquarius. 'New Age' is a reaction against the artificiality of materialism that has ignored and starved the body-spirit nature of human beings. In its feminist form, it is a reaction against domination by the male ego through economic or cultural imperialism. In its ecological form, it is a reaction against scientific and industrial abuse of nature. In its astrological form, it is a return to awareness of the forces and rhythms of the elements. In its psychological form, it is an opening up to and an abandonment to the flow of unconscious forces through dreams, etc. Its religious aspect may take the form of eastern pantheistic meditation, theosophy, spiritism, white or black magic, or Druid revivalism. In the Church, there are mild expressions of it in some courses at retreat houses, and in creationist theology.

The creationist theologian Matthew Fox spells out a number of things that all Christians need to hear. However, having rightly raised these issues, he offers remedies that I believe are ultimately anti-Christian. He rejects theism on the grounds that it 'kills God and the soul alike by preaching a God "out there"'. All theisms, he says, are about subject/object relationships to God, which are a bad thing. He wishes to replace theism with panentheism, which means 'God is in everything and everything is in God'.

The *Oxford Dictionary* defines theism as: 'Belief in existence of a god supernaturally revealed to man, and sustaining a personal relation to his creatures'. Orthodox Christianity holds these two truths together: God is in all things and God is distinct from all things. Yet Fox seems to imply that by uniting ourselves to 'all things', we infuse energy, wholeness and God. This is the fallacy of the New Age. It becomes worship of nature, a new paganism.

There is a subtle reason why people prefer to think of God as merely a power, or a formless life-force flowing through the universe: there are no demands – one is not challenged to relate to an energy in the same way one is challenged to relate to a person. C. S. Lewis put it like this: 'The Pantheist's God does nothing, demands nothing. He is there if you wish for Him, like a book on a shelf. He will not pursue you. There is no danger that at any time heaven or earth should feel awe at His glance. But Christ the Creator King is *there*. And his intervening presence is terribly startling to discover.'

Magic, even white magic, uses elemental powers to control another person's life: Christian prayer seeks to set a person free from all that prevents them being their true self. New Ageism abandons the self to elemental powers: Christianity harnesses the self to Christ, who creates and redeems the elemental powers. Celtic Christianity says matter is holy, but matter is not God. We need to relate to every organism, but through Christ. As we do this, he filters out what is destructive in us, keeping the space that gives each their distinctive identity. This enables communion. There is no communion when there is absorption. Celtic Christianity (and this may have been the real message of Pelagius) does not teach that all humans inherit original guilt, in the sense of a curse that is put upon us which makes us automatons, but it does face up to the seriousness and the scope of the flaw that is sin. The whole cosmos is fallen. Our unconscious self is fallen. All needs to be redeemed.

Celtic Christians did not fall into the trap of blaming either devils or pagan beliefs for evils that belonged to the sphere of human responsibility. Fursey, the Irish monk who spread Christianity in East Anglia, was given a vision when he was ill. He looked down on the earth and saw four terrible fires that threatened to destroy it. The four fires were: Falsehood, Covetousness, Discord and Exploitation. For the rest of his life he fought passionately to save people from such a fate. The abiding memory of this vision made him sweat every time he warned someone to make restitution in the light of the coming judgement. It is thought that the book of his visions (which is now lost) gave rise to a new genre of literature that came to a climax with Dante's *Paradise Lost* and *Paradise Regained*.

Restitution was the hallmark of the penitentials that Celtic church leaders popularised throughout Europe. Unlike the continental Church, where confession was made to a priest, and absolution received, without restitution having to be made to the wronged person, the Celts *based* penitence upon restitution. Sin had to be dealt with, wrongs had to be put right. The aim was that the relationship with the wronged person was restored.

Christian leaders such as David, in Wales, produced penitentials that matched a penance to the nature of the sin. For example, a cleric who got drunk was to fast for forty days on bread and water. The penitentials used in Ireland in the sixth and seventh centuries were schedules drawn up for a confessor, or *anmchara*.[7] The *anmchara's* job was to apply the appropriate cure to the soul's disease. The seventh-century Cummean in his 'prologue on the medicine for the salvation of souls' states: 'The eight principal vices . . . shall be healed by the eight remedies that are their contraries.' The vices were: gluttony, fornication, greed, temper, self-pity, laziness, vainglory and pride.

We learn from Columbanus' Rule that if someone stole something from their neighbour then they had to restore it. If they had stolen so many things over too long a period to be able to pay them all back, then they had to live on bread and water for a specified period, and give a proportion of income from their work for the relief of the poor. These are principles which, if they were applied regardless of whether they were cost-effective, could transform our society as much as they did Celtic society. In the ceaseless struggle between good and evil, the Celtic Christians never lost the link between confession and restitution.

The penitentials show that the Celtic Church in Britain and Ireland was the first to make private penance a general practice. They must have influenced some of the prayers of confession such as those in the Book of Cerne (the worship book of the Celtic monastery at Cerne, on the River Boyne, Ireland). One such prayer to God as 'doctor of the soul' has an almost exact parallel in a later Irish poem:

> Guard my eyes for me, Jesus Son of Mary, lest seeing another's
>   wealth make me covetous . . .
> Guard for me my ears lest they hearken to slander . . .
> Guard for me my tongue lest they listen to slander . . .
> Guard for me my hands, that they be not stretched out for
>   quarrelling . . .
> Guard for me my feet upon the gentle earth of Ireland,
> Lest, bent on profitless errands, they abandon rest.[8]

Penance was only one arrow in the bow of these archers in the spiritual conflict. There was an over-arching progression in the Rules of Life of the different communities, which were designed to help everyone advance in the spiritual offensive. For example, the three stages in Columbanus' Rule were: 1 nakedness and disdain of riches; 2 purging of vices; 3, the most perfect and perpetual love of God.

One day, a Scottish minister, whose training had led him to dismiss the supernatural, discovered that even church members were going for healing to people who had a greater power, such as spiritist mediums. Something turned inside him: 'Why should people go to almost anyone except Christ's ministers to be cured?' he asked himself, 'from now on I am going to confront every kind of evil in the name of Christ.' In doing this, he was treading in the steps of his Scottish father in the faith, Columba. Columba used every means to overcome evil with good, and, above all, the cross of Christ. He frequently used the sign of the cross, which was called the saving sign, to keep away evil. Before the cows were milked the sign would be made over the milk pail; the seed was crossed that the crop might escape the spells of the evil one. Lucy Menzies writes: 'The supernatural nature of the sacred sign appealed to the Highlanders, and was possibly the origin of the custom of erecting crosses, to wage endless war against the powers of evil and to commemorate at certain spots the victory of Christ over the devil.'[9] Every Christian, at their baptism, is called to take up their cross daily, and to engage in the eternal struggle.

The Celtic Church was marked by holiness, but not pietism. The Celtic saints withdrew from the world, not to retreat from the struggle with reality, but to confront it. To them, true religion meant a robust intervention in the affairs of the world, a willingness to counterattack the powers of evil – to accept, if necessary, martyrdom. That was the way of Christ and of most of his apostles. It was not war, but it was, in Emerson's phrase, 'the moral equivalent of war'. Without this ceaseless struggle, war itself cannot be averted.

A Prayer
> In the strength of the Warrior of God,
> I oppose all that pollutes;
> In the eye of the Face of God
> I expose all that deceives;
> In the energy of the Servant of God
> I bind up all that is broken.

A Response
> I will fight daily against sin, evil and the devil.

13

The Encircling Three

'Jesus said: "Go then to all peoples everywhere . . . baptise them in the name of the Father, the Son, and the Holy Spirit"' (Matthew 28:19).

The author of Matthew's Gospel did not intend the Church to regard the Trinity as a formula for a one-off occasion of baptism. He had in mind people's immersion in the Trinity as a way of life. The Celts truly lived this way. God was infinite yet intimate; he was holy yet homely. He was sovereign and could not be bargained with, yet he was alongside them in their everyday needs.

Many people feel the world is out of control, that there is no one 'out there'; they feel adrift. The Christian idea that three Persons run the world is a revolutionary discovery.

This discovery was expressed at Jesus' baptism. There was the Father in the form of the voice from heaven, the Son in the form of Jesus the man, and the Spirit in the form of the dove that settled on Jesus (Mark 1: 9–11); it was thereafter expressed at every Christian's baptism (Matthew 28:19). Irenaeus helped the Church to draw forth the fuller implications of this truth: the relationship between these three Persons, and the part each played in creating and re-creating the universe and human history.

First, God the Father, uncreated, who cannot be defined or seen, Creator of the Universe. Second, the Word of God, the Son of God, Christ Jesus our Saviour, who became human among humans, to be seen and touched, to cause life to spring up, and to establish full communion between God and humanity. And third, the Holy Spirit, by whom forebears received revelations, who was poured out in a new way upon humanity, to renew it all over the earth, and to bring into union with God.[1]

According to tradition, Patrick put this revolutionary teaching at the centre of his mission. 'St Patrick's Breastplate' makes this clear: 'I bind unto myself the name, the strong name of The Trinity; by invocation of the same, the Three in One, and One in Three, of whom all nature has creation; Eternal Father, Spirit, Word . . .'[2]

Later tradition suggests that Patrick used the three-leafed shamrock to teach that the one God was also Three. A poem inspired by this tradition has recently been revived in the form of a song by Sammy Horner, the Celtic singer:

> The Three are the One and the One is the Three,
> Blessed Father Son Spirit, the blessed Trinity.
>
> Three seams in this garment, one garment I wear
> Three leaves on the shamrock from the soil that I tear
> Three joints in my finger yet one finger there
> Blessed Father Son Spirit yet one God I serve.
>
> She's a wife and a mother and a daughter in one
> I'm a father a husband and also a son
> And the water can be the steam or the snow
> Blessed Father Son Spirit yet one God I know.
>
> Now no tongue can tell, no language explain
> The Greatness of God, or his fullness of being
> and though it remains a great mystery
> You're a Father, a Saviour and comfort to me.[3]

Columba, like Patrick, had to confront the false teachings of the Druids. He is reported as saying: 'My Druid is Christ the Son of God, Christ, Son of Mary, the Great Abbot, The Father, the Son and the Holy Spirit.' I have always assumed that when Columba made the sign of the cross, as he frequently did, the threefold movement was also a sign of the Trinity. This has certainly become part of the Celtic, and indeed of the Catholic, tradition. The prayers and sayings of the nineteenth-century Scottish highlanders collected by Alexander Carmichael indicate that a profound understanding of the Trinity, whom they addressed as the Three, had taken root:

> The Three who are over my head,
> The Three who are under my tread,
> The Three who are over me here,
> The Three who are over me there,

The Three who are in the earth near,
The Three who are up in the air,
The Three who in heaven do dwell,
The Three in the great ocean swell,
Pervading Three, O be with me.

The Three be about your head
The Three be about your breast,

The Three be about your body,
Each night and each day,
In the encompassment of the Three
Throughout your life long.

I lie down tonight,
With the Triune of my strength,
With the Father, with Jesus,
With the Spirit of might.[4]

Pagan and Christian Celts often wrote in triads. This instinctive mirroring of the ultimate nature of reality has been reflected in recent worship resource materials produced by the Community of Aidan and Hilda. Its Trinity triads begin:

Power of all powers (R) *We worship you*
Light of all lights (R) *We worship you*
Life of all lives (R) *We worship you*

Source of all life (R) *We acknowledge you*
Saviour of all life (R) *We acknowledge you*
Sustainer of all life (R) *we acknowledge you*[5]

A Prayer
May the love of the Three give birth to a new community;
May the uniting of the Three give birth to a new solidarity;
May the flowing of the Three give birth to a new creativity;
May the oneness of the Three give birth to a new unity;
May the glory of the Three give birth to a new society.

A Response
I will often immerse people, places and myself in the joy, power and protecting presence of the Sacred Three.

14

The Wild Goose

'The wind blows wherever it wishes . . . it is like that with everyone who is born of the Spirit' (John 3:8).

It is all too easy for the Church, as an institution, to try to tame God's Spirit. The Bible pictures the Holy Spirit as untameable – as wind, fire, or a dove. The dove was not, as we often imagine it, so domesticated that it never flies outside the comfort of its dovecot. The rock doves of the Bible flew in from the wild and back out into the wild. The Celts' use of the wild goose as a symbol of God's Spirit captured this biblical sense of wildness.

God has built places of wildness into both nature and human nature. How many 'way out' people, who have dismissed the Church as unadventurous, realise that Christianity offers a route to a true wildness that does not destroy?

John Bell and Graham Maule have written:

The Celtic monks, knowing that same restlessness and provocation which issues from the Almighty, depicted the Holy Spirit both as a dove *and* a wild goose. But where in our contemporary devotions are there glimpses that God, in the twentieth century, can be expected to surprise, contradict, upset or rile us in order that the Kingdom may come?[1]

It will repay us to become familiar with some of our Celtic forebears' experiences of the wild goose or the wild dove. In Wales, early in the sixth century, Bishop Dubricius and St Illtyd came to ordain Samson as a deacon and two other men as priests. As the candidates prostrated themselves in prayer, the two ordaining ministers saw a dove fly through the open window and remain above Samson's head, with wings outstretched, and without any flapping. It stayed there a long time while they went to and fro during the

122 *Exploring Celtic Spirituality*

worship, until the bishop placed his hand over Samson to ordain him. At that moment, the dove perched on Samson's right shoulder and stayed there until he came to receive Holy Communion. Only these two holy men saw the dove. Filled with wonder, they took it as a sign of God's renewing power in a person of his choice.[2]

Anointings of the Holy Spirit in Celtic times did not come to order, but they were not in short supply, and they had an unexpected impact. We noted earlier that a bishop who was about to profess Brigid as a nun was so overwhelmed by the sheet of flame he saw above her that he read out the words for the consecration of a bishop by mistake!

Patrick experienced the wild goose in an out-of-the-body vision:

I saw Him praying in me, and He it was as it were within my body, and I heard Him above me, that is, above the inner man, and there He was praying mightily with groanings. And meanwhile I was astonished and pondered who it could be that was praying in me. But at the end of the prayer He spoke as if He were the Spirit. And so I awoke, and remembered that the Apostle says, 'The Spirit helps the infirmities of our prayers; but the Spirit himself asks for us with unspeakable groanings [Romans 8:23] which cannot be expressed in words'.[3]

Adamnan's biography of Columba includes a chapter entitled 'The visit of the Holy Spirit which continued for three whole days and nights'. Columba was fasting alone in an island house. Through the chinks in the doors and windows at night, brilliant rays of light and melodies of praise poured forth, and amazing revelations about the Scriptures, the past and the future were given to him.[4]

The sentiments of a song by the band Iona, 'I say a prayer that the Wild Goose will come to me', are being echoed by many voices today.

I respond to the opportunism, the wildness, the freedom of the spirit of these Celts (Russ Parker).

It is the work of the Holy Spirit to disturb a man or an institution that is becoming settled or stiff (Alec Vidler).

The Holy Spirit is not a tame bird, kept in a clean cage, to be released for short bursts at charismatic meetings . . . The Holy Spirit makes his habitation in some of the wildest and darkest places this world has to offer . . . The Holy Spirit is wonderfully free, able to go to the dark places of our own lives, for healing, to the dark unvisited places of our churches, and to the dark and demon-infested places of our society (Michael Mitton).

Then I saw the wild geese flying in fair formation to their passes
  in Inchicore
And I knew that these wings would outwear the wings of war
And a man's simple thoughts outlive the day's loud lying.
Don't fear, don't fear, I said to my soul.
The Bedlam of Time is an empty bucket rattled,
'Tis you who will say in the end who best battles.
Only they who fly home to God have flown at all
(Patrick Kavanagh).

Catch the Bird of Heaven
Look again tomorrow and he will be gone.
Ah, the Bird of Heaven! Follow where the Bird has gone
If you want to find him, keep on travelling on.
Lock him in religion. Gold and frankincense and myrrh
Carry to his prison, but he will be gone.
Temple made of marble, beak and feather made of gold,
Bell and book and candle, but he will be gone
Bell and book and candle cannot hold him any more
Still the Bird is flying, as he did before.
Ah, the Bird of Heaven! Follow where the Bird has gone
If you want to find him, keep on travelling on (Sidney Carter).

A Prayer
  Great Spirit, Wild Goose of the Almighty
  Be my eye in the dark places;
  Be my flight in the trapped places;
  Be my host in the wild places;
  Be my brood in the barren places;
  Be my formation in the lost places.

A Response
  Seek to be open to the unexpected promptings of God's Spirit.

15

Signs and Wonders

'Believers will be given power to perform miracles: they will drive out demons in my name; they will speak in strange tongues . . .' (Mark 16:17).

Signs and wonders marked the life of Jesus, as the Gospels frequently portray; and also of his disciples, as the Acts of the Apostles makes clear. These signs are not a divine marketing device; Jesus warned people against that sort of thing (Matthew 16:4). Such signs and wonders are what happens when a Superior Being is invited to invade a fallen created life. They are given to meet a need and to give glory to God.

The resurrection of Christ and the coming of the Holy Spirit at the first Christian Pentecost certainly brought a huge burst of signs and wonders in their wake. However, the dogma that this was limited to the time of the apostles, and became unnecessary once the New Testament was completed, contradicts both the teaching of the Bible and the experience of God's people. The alternative ending to Mark's Gospel given above (Mark 16:17) represents the early Church's belief about this matter. It is clear that Jesus expected all future believers to be channels of signs and wonders.

Christianity came to the pagan Celts by way of signs and wonders. Ninian's pioneer mission in Galloway towards the end of the fourth century was bitterly opposed by the local king, until he was struck by a disease that cost him his sight. The king asked Ninian to forgive him. Following Christ's example, Ninian not only forgave him, but restored his sight. Thus the royal doors became opened to the gospel in north-west Britain.

Ninian's Community of the Shining House radiated God's love to the area, but one young member who had committed a serious offence ran away, taking with him Ninian's staff. He went to sea, but the leaky boat began to sink. The runaway was brought to his knees in a deeply felt change of heart, and then struck the boatside with Ninian's staff. Instantly, the leak stopped. He returned a changed person, imbued with awe at the signs and wonders God can work.[1]

Columba spent little time arguing with potential converts. His approach was: 'You say you have power? Well, whatever you have got, I bring a greater power, that of God, the Almighty Trinity.'

Columba's biographer, Adamnan, compiled a *Life of Columba*, which he divided into three books entitled respectively: 1 Prophetic Revelations, 2 Miraculous Powers, and 3 Visions of Angels. Columba's life and work were bathed in the supernatural from beginning to end. The second book begins with an account of Columba, like Jesus, turning water into wine. Water featured in a number of Columba's miracles. On one occasion, a couple asked him to baptise their infant, but there was no water near. Columba felt that God led him to a particular rock where he knelt in prayer for some time. Water then gushed out and the baby was more than adequately baptised.[2]

Columba learned this approach from the Church that Patrick bequeathed to Ireland. Before Patrick went out to crusade, he experienced signs and wonders in his own inner life. Patrick had his critics and some judged him to be a failure, but he would not hide the signs and wonders that were a witness – not to him, but to his Lord: 'Let him who will, laugh and insult, I will not be silent, nor will I hide the signs and wonders which were ministered to me by the Lord, many years before they came to pass, as He who knew all things before the world began.'[3]

The Victorian biographers of Celtic saints attempted to de-mythologise the realm of the supernatural in the saints' lives, while the saints' medieval biographers assumed that each saint must have run the whole gamut of signs and wonders even if they hadn't! The truth is that, even if we only consider the broad brush strokes of these biographies, we cannot doubt that the men and women they portray were at home in the world of the supernatural. The Life of Brendan illustrates this: '. . . and after raising of dead men, healing lepers, blind, deaf, lame and all kinds of sick folk . . . after expelling demons and vices . . . after performance of mighty works and miracles too numerous to mention, St Brendan drew near to the day of his death'.[4]

Bede's catalogue of miracles

Bede was not a man to exaggerate, nor to give more credit to the
Celtic way than the facts demanded, yet he had to admit that even
men such as Aidan and Cuthbert, whose lives were accessible to
close scrutiny, performed signs and wonders:

> How great the merits of Aidan were, was made manifest by the
> all-seeing Judge, with the testimony of miracles, whereof it will
> suffice to mention three as a memorial . . . Inside the monastery
> the man of God [Cuthbert] performed more and more signs and
> wonders.[5]

A cursory glance through Bede's chapter headings alone is
enough to reveal how awesome were the signs and wonders in
those days:

> How, among innumerable other miraculous cures wrought by
> the Cross . . . a certain youth had his lame arm healed . . . How a
> traveller's horse was restored and a young girl cured of the palsy
> . . . Of a boy cured of an ague . . . Of the signs that were shown
> from heaven when the mother of that congregation departed . . .
> How a pestilential mortality ceased through the intercession of
> king Oswald . . . How Ethelwald calmed a tempest when the
> brethren were in danger at sea . . . How Bishop John, by his
> prayers, healed a sick man . . . recovered one of his servants
> from death . . .[6]

Visions were given, people healed, devils cast out, holy oil
calmed the waves of a storm, and a whole town was saved from
pagan attack because of the prayers of Aidan.

The Christian Church today is again realising the power of God
through prayer – for healing, for evangelising, for guidance, and
for calming inner storms in people's lives. We need to appropriate
even more of 'his incomparably great power for us who believe'
(Ephesians 1:19).

A Prayer

Great Father of the blood-red moon and of the falling stars;
Great Saviour of the miraculous birth and of the rising from
   death;
Great Spirit of the creators and the seers;
Come in sovereign power
into our dreams
into our thoughts
into our mouths
into our bodies
into our actions
Till we become His sign, and presence, and wonder.

A Response

I make myself wholly available for you to work through me in
signs and wonders for your glory and not mine.

16

The Prophetic Spirit

'I only say what the Father has instructed me to say . . .
He who comes from God listens to God's words'
(John 8:28, 47).

Jesus had such an intimate relationship with his Father that he knew what God wanted him to see, do and say in every situation. That, says Jesus, will also be the aim of everyone who tries to come to things from God's angle. This prophetic basis of living has been on God's agenda for his people from the beginning. He has always wanted his people to respond to his voice. We are now in the 'age of the Holy Spirit', when God will pour his Spirit on everyone (Acts 2:17). Not everyone is called to the special ministry of the prophet, but something of the prophetic spirit is available to everybody.

The art of listening has been largely lost today. In order to recover it we must become attentive to the inner voice. The Celts had a well-developed sixth sense. This sense of augury or *frith* was thought to be inherited by some of the Highlanders whom Alexander Carmichael met in the last century, and we need to develop this too. But the prophetic life of the Celtic Christians was much more than a sixth sense; it was God's supernatural gifts being invited into holy lives as they were needed.

'Words of knowledge' or prophecy come to people who are familiar with the supernatural, and only the most dramatic examples get recorded in accounts of such men and women of God. Yet the larger the base of the pyramid, the higher it will reach. In other words, the more people who become familiar with God's words in everyday life, the greater will be the number of historically memorable words from God.

The traditional image of a prophet is that of an old wise man.

Although God raises up prophetic people of any age, there is sense in this image for there are many pitfalls in prophecy. For example, it is easy to project an unconscious wish from our own ego in the name of God. If lives are rushed, or cluttered, much that is purely human will get mixed up with that which comes from God.

The Celts prophesied out of purity. They could live in solitude, and face their own 'shadow', as Carl Jung termed it. That is also why they did not prophesy routinely; prophecy was fresh, original, true.

A child was born in Ulster in the year 453 who was to become known as St Brigid of Kildare. She had the gift of prophecy, and foretold the birth of Columba in these words: 'a young scion will be born in the north and will become a great tree whose top will reach over Erin and Alban'. How this must have lifted succeeding generations of Christians who might otherwise have lowered their sights after the Church's initial burst of energy. And that is one of the purposes of prophecy: to build God's people up.

Significant life experiences became a focus for prophecy, particularly births. Before Brendan's birth in 484, his mother dreamed that her womb was full of pure gold. On the night of his birth, Erc, the local bishop, saw, in a vision, the village in one enormous blaze. Realising this was a child marked out for a special destiny, Erc arranged for a nun to bring Brendan up. Similarly, Eithne, Columba's mother, had a dream while awaiting his birth. An angel told her she would have a son who would 'blossom for heaven and be of so beautiful a character that he would be reckoned among his own people as one of the prophets of God who would lead innumerable souls to the heavenly country'.[1]

It was said that one day Columba's guardian angel asked him which virtues he most longed to possess. Columba chose wisdom, chastity and prophecy. His life was marked by prophetic powers to an unusual degree. Columba had second sight, and 'words of knowledge' brought an effective touch to his ministry on many occasions. He once acknowledged that 'heaven has granted to some to see on occasion in their minds clearly and surely, the whole of earth and sea'. Once when his friends were keen to go out fishing in the River Boyle, he said, 'No fish will be found in the river today or tomorrow, but on the third day I will send you and you will find two large river salmon.' This they did.

Monks at Iona decided to postpone welcome preparations for guests because it seemed obvious that no boat could cross to the island during such a stormy period. But Columba told them, 'The Lord has given a calm evening in this tempest for a certain holy man who will arrive before evening.' The guest, St Cainnech, duly arrived.

Columba prophesied with great power and precision right up to the end of his life. His world-famous prophecy about Iona is coming true after more than a thousand years:

> In Iona of my heart, Iona of my love,
> Instead of monk's voice shall be the lowing of cows;
> but ere the world shall come to an end,
> Iona shall be as it was.

Prophecies were practical

Prophecies also focused on the practical necessities of life. When Aidan's friend Utta was about to begin a long journey to escort Northumbria's queen back from Kent, he asked for Aidan's prayers. He received a prophecy and some oil, as well as prayer! Aidan told the departing group: 'When you board your ship you will meet storms and adverse winds. Remember to pour this oil on to the sea; the winds will drop at once, and the sea will become calm, and bring you the right way home.' The sailors were almost shipwrecked before they recalled the prophecy and used the oil, which worked immediately.

Sometimes prophecies were related to a person's calling, and sometimes to their dying. The first time that Boisil, of Melrose Monastery, saw the teenage Cuthbert, he prophesied: 'Here is the servant of the Lord'. Boisil foretold the arrival of the plague to Abbot Eata three years before it came, and also that he himself would perish. He said that Eata, however, would not die as a result of plague, but would perish from dysentery. This all came to pass.

There was a prophetic edge in everything that Cuthbert did, though he did not regard himself as being at the forefront of prophetic ministry. He said, 'I have known many abbots who for purity of mind and depth of prophetic power have far surpassed my poor self – Boisil for example . . . while he was instructing me he prophesied my whole future accurately. One of these prophecies has yet to happen: Would to God it might not!' He was referring to Boisil's prophecy that he would one day be a bishop. Cuthbert only acceded to pressure for him to become a bishop because it had been prophesied by such a holy man as Boisil.

The spirit of prophecy dries up when would-be prophets become bureaucrats. There is no record of prelates such as Wilfred, who were patronising towards the Celtic Christians, prophesying. As in Amos' day, when 'there was a famine of hearing the words of God', so in some parts of the Church today there is a famine of hearing God's words.

Yet there is also a rising counter dynamic. Certain prophetic figures in the United States have had a Columba-like accuracy in the detail of their prophecies, though they may not have been refined in the disciplines of Columba. Marc Dupont, an associate minister in the Toronto Vineyard Church, offered this prophecy at a conference for church leaders at St Andrew's Church Chorleywood in September 1994:

> God looks at the residue and deposits of glory of what he's established, and God is going to touch the deep wells – and these wells are going to spring up again. I believe that at least one third of the Anglican churches in Great Britain are going to begin to burst with evangelism and the power of the Holy Spirit in a new way . . . I think you are at a time when the Lord is saying 'Dig up those old visions; dig up those old dreams that God has given you . . . They are going to be refined because you will no longer operate out of pride or human inertia but you will go forth by the Spirit of God.'

Christians can take three stances towards the idea of 'tuning in'. They may tune in to all unseen vibrations: this enslaves the Spirit. They may cut out all such tunings-in: this can quench the Spirit. Or they may die to the desire to tune in, but then receive the gift of redeemed tuning. This is the testimony of a number of Christians I know.

Discernment of three separate strands in the prophetic process has helped some churches to develop a more mature prophetic ministry. There is the original subject matter (e.g. a picture or word) that the recipient offers. There is the weighing and the interpretation of it, which discerning people in church leadership oversee. There is the application, when the Holy Spirit may convict an individual or a group.

The value of prophecy can be recognised by church leaders who have found themselves in an institutionalised role. The Advisory Council on Relations of Bishops and Religious Communities in the

Church of England states: 'Religious Communities are independent associations expressing by their life and work a prophetic role which complements, and sometimes challenges, the life of the church as a whole.'[2]

> Because of our belief in God as Spirit
> we choose to affirm and encourage
> the prophetic voices
> that recognise both the sin
> and the need of our time.[3]

Britain – a listening land

> So much noise –
> Tumult of traffic,
> Roar of machines
> Shots in the night,
> The words, words, words
> Of a million viewpoints.

> So much noise –
> Drowning the cry of need
> Behind the words
> We speak,
> Drowning the voice of the prophets
> And the heartbreak in the wind.

> From the everlasting stillness
> At the heart of the universe
> A voice speaks, loving, merciful, wide,
> Full of grace and strength.
> The voice of God the Father,
> Giving to those who listen
> Hope for tomorrow,
> Tranquillity in turmoil
> An end to loneliness,
> The promise of joy in battle.

> He speaks, not only to the few
> With time for quietness,
> But to us, in the rush of life
> With the noise of humanity
> Battering our ears,
> When we listen, He speaks.

Britain, a listening land
Listening to one another,
Hearing the voices of the prophets
And the heartbreak in the wind,
Listening to that Voice
Which gives wisdom.[4]

A Prayer

Voice of the great God, come in thunder,
Voice of the great God, come in the gap;
Voice of the great God, come in the visions;
Voice of the great God, come in the sap;
Voice of the great God, come in the silence;
Voice of the great God, come in my lap.

A Response

I pledge to give time to listening to God and becoming aware of his voice; to grow in prophetic ministry, speaking prophetically to his servants and to those who do not yet know him.

17

Healing

'Heal the sick' (Luke 10:9).

The same New Testament word is used for 'to save' and 'to heal'. Jesus came to cure people, and often this included their bodies, their minds and their emotions. The Church has always taught that Jesus' healing ministry is continued in the Church today. However, in periods when the Church has become bureaucratic, healing has sometimes been reserved for the clergy and formal sacraments. Even in these periods, though, healings took place through people who became known as saints.

Jesus taught his followers (not just the apostles) to heal the sick. He told them to teach all future believers to do all he had commanded them to do (Matthew 28:20) – and this included healing the sick.

This century, most of the world's churches are restoring the ministry of healing to its rightful place in the Church's life. In the Church of England, for example, an Archbishops' Commission issued a report in 1958 entitled *The Church's Healing Ministry*, and later Bishop Maurice Maddocks founded the Acorn Healing Trust. The foundation period of the Church in Britain and Ireland offers some useful insights into the restoration of this ministry.

The level of expectation for healing had dropped to zero in the Church once it became the official religion of the Empire. This was so in Wales, even after Illtyd and Dubricius had brought in a new holiness at the monastery at Llantwit. When one of the monks was dying from a snake bite, his brothers gathered round to practise ministry to the dying. Samson, however, who was a deeply attentive Bible student, assumed that since Jesus and his followers healed sick people, so should he. He requested Illtyd to allow him to lay hands on his dying brother and pray for recovery.

At first, the holy Illtyd thought Samson's motive must be to rival the magic charms of the Druids, but he acquiesced. The brother was restored to health, and so the healing ministry began to revive in the Welsh Church.

There is no suggestion that in the Celtic Church healing was restricted to ministers, or even to adults. Brigid took the initiative in healing while she was still a youngster. Her pagan father's attendant was once taken ill while she was travelling with them. Brigid fetched water from a well, prayed over it, and gave it to the attendant to drink. It tasted like ale; so he drank it all, and recovered. Later, when she was the leader of the monastery at Kildare, the sick came – and many were healed; lepers, though not cured of their leprosy, were given barrels full of apples; and Christian workers came for advice on what today we would call inner healing.

Brigid developed faith-sharing teams to minister in churches, not all of which maintained an effective healing ministry; Easter was a special opportunity, because many extra people came to church. One Easter, Brigid found herself in a church packed with needy people, and with none of the staff willing to offer healing. So Brigid ministered herself, and that same day a leper, a blind person, a consumptive and a deranged person were all reported healed.

Healing is wholeness

We get no hint of triumphalism or false claims about healing in the Celtic Church. They knew the ravages of plague only too well. They understood healing as wholeness, the restoration of harmony with oneself, the environment, God. But belief in a general wholeness did not mean they shied away from the healing of physical ailments. They always healed in the power and name of Christ; they boldly used gifts of faith, prophecy or material artefacts from a place or person of healing, such as oil, water, moss or wood, that carried the healing power from God to the sick. These all brought a marvellous crop of physical healings.

By invoking the name of Christ, Columba

> healed the disorders of various sick persons . . . For either by his merely stretching out his holy hand or by sprinkling of the sick with water blessed by him, or by their touching even the

hem of his cloak, or by their receiving his blessing on anything, as for instance on bread or salt, and dipping it in water, those who believed recovered perfect health.[1]

Cuthbert himself was struck down by the plague that was killing thousands:

> The monks spent the whole night praying for his recovery. Next morning one of them told Cuthbert of this vigil. 'Then what am I lying here for?' Cuthbert responded. 'God will certainly have heard the prayers of so many good men. Fetch my shoes and stick.' He got up there and then and tried to walk with the stick. Day by day his strength came back until he was quite recovered; only the swelling on the thigh seemed to move inwards, and for almost the whole of his life he was troubled with some internal pain.[2]

Cuthbert did not cease to perform miracles of healing even when he was on Farne Island, and far removed from people. One of his friends, who had charge of a large number of nuns, had long been ill, and she was unable to move except on all fours. She had given up hope of getting any help from doctors. One day, someone came with a linen cloth sent by Cuthbert, in answer to her prayers. She put it on and next morning was able to stand up straight. Two days later, she was completely well.

Anointing with oil was a familiar practice. One nun was seriously ill; she was seized up with pains in the head, and all down one side – so much so that the doctors had given up hope. Cuthbert's companions begged him to heal her. Full of pity, he anointed her with holy oil. She began to improve from that very moment, and in a few days she was completely recovered.

After he became a bishop, Cuthbert was asked to visit the home of one of King Ecgfrith's bodyguards, one of whose servants was very ill, unable to sleep and barely breathing. Cuthbert blessed some water, and a fellow-servant poured it down the man's throat three times. He fell into a deep sleep. The following morning he was restored to full health. The fellow servant was Baldhelm, who later reported: 'It is sweeter than honey to have to recount Cuthbert's miracles to any who care to know them; he told me this one himself.'[3]

When Jesus healed people, he sometimes gave a direct command, rebuke or action. This aspect of healing ministry is amusingly reflected in these prayers that Alexander Carmichael heard and wrote down:

> Extinction to your microbe,
> Extinction to your swelling,
> Peace be to your breats,
> The peace of the King of power.
>
> I repel you, O stye,
> By guidance of Father.
> *(Thrust a needle)*
>
> I repel you, O stye,
> By guidance of Son!
> *(Thrust)*
>
> I repel you, O stye,
> By guidance of Spirit!
> *(Thrust)*[4]

A Prayer
Healing of the Three be with you;
Healing of the Three be in your body;
Healing of the Three be in your mind;
Healing of the Three be in your spirit.

A Response
I will pray for the sick to be healed.

18

A Church without Walls

'The believers . . . enjoying the goodwill of all the people'
(Acts 2:44, 47).

Solzhenitsyn believes that the world is at a turning point: 'East
and West are sick of the same disease of materialism which
fragments communities, families and persons.' He believes that
the answer lies in a rebirth of *Sobornost*, a communal life based
on moral and spiritual values, which grows around an unsullied
Church.

Christ chose twelve apostles who were 'of the people', and they
had the rough edges knocked off them by travelling, working and
praying together. The apostles constantly use the word 'we' when
preaching to their fellow citizens – they assumed a human solidarity
with them.

Often, twentieth-century Christians are not in touch with the
human roots they share with those in the neighbourhood. Yet
God's Spirit is speaking into this situation, calling all Christians
to become a 'Church for the unchurched', or a 'Church without walls'.

The last time that Britain or Ireland had a truly endogenous
Church was in Celtic times. The Celtic churches were of the
people and of the land. They felt the pain of the folk among
whom they existed. This gave the churches an innate authority
within the community; it gave their worship unfading conviction.
The Church had depth, but was not overlaid with clutter; it had
breadth, but was not sidetracked into compartments. Once the
initial evangelist had done his work, the Church threw up its own
natural leaders.

The Celtic 'Church without walls' held out three great principles
that are ripe for our adoption today:

140 *Exploring Celtic Spirituality*

The first principle is that of human solidarity. When Celtic monks crossed the seas to evangelise, they did not go as isolated individuals; instead, they often went as a team of twelve, dependent upon the friendship of people for their food and shelter. Thus from the beginning of a church being planted, it was of the people.

Patrick set an example of being in solidarity with the Irish people to whom he had been sent: 'Though I could wish to leave them and proceed to the Britons, as to my country and parents . . . Christ the Lord . . . commanded me to come, and to be with them for the rest of my life.'[1]

This principle of solidarity with the people meant that the Church in Ireland did not develop a ghetto mentality; instead, it travelled along the social and cultural corridors of its citizens where these were not opposed to Christianity. In Patrick's Ireland, 'the church was simply a series of Christian communities bound together on the family principle which formed the characteristic feature of the Celtic national life'.[2]

A social focus

The second principle is hospitality to the people. In seventh-century Northumbria, the Christian Church gathered all the people of the locality together for feasts, in which they were caught up together in the human joys of celebration and relaxation:

> It was the time for a night of feasting . . . a time when the people forgot the hard conditions of their lives and joyed in one another's company; in rustic mirth, in music and dancing and the telling of tales told or song of the bards. The farm-workers and folk from the village gathered in the great barn of the monastery. The space round the fire was left empty for the visiting bard.[3]

At the monastery at Whitby, in a dream God told the herdsman, Caedmon, to start singing the stories of the Bible. The Abbess Hilda brought him into the monastery as a monk, where he began to sing the stories of the Bible – and no doubt often left the folk spellbound at occasions such as the community feasts. Caedmon used the milieu and dialect with which the people felt at home.

David fostered hospitality towards the people of Wales. He put a stress 'on loving-kindness in the small things of daily life'. In doing so he was attempting to restore his shattered land, rebuilding it as a network of communities based on love of God and love of neighbour, and held together by a common faith.

One modern Welsh poet imagines how David

> brought the church to our homes, and took bread from the pantry and bad wine from the cellar, and stood behind the table like a tramp so as not to hide the wonder of the Sacrifice from us. After the communion we chatted by the fireside, and he talked to us about God's natural order, the person, the family, the nation and the society of nations, and the Cross keeping us from turning any one of them into a god.[4]

The third principle is the renunciation of power. The practice at Lindisfarne of the bishop living as a monk under the authority of the abbot insured that bishops were not corrupted either by worldly goods (they were not allowed to own anything) or by the possibility of abuse of power. Now that the Church of England is intent on removing checks and balances to episcopal power (such as the right of a parson to remain the shepherd of his or her flock for life), the need to build in accountability for bishops assumes a high priority.

F. E. Warren, the author of a weighty compendium of Celtic liturgies, warns us that Bede, through whose writings we gain so much knowledge of the Celtic Church, 'yields, as so many have done after him, to the hateful temptation of identifying the work of God with a human conquest'.[5] The Celts never did that. They did not use worldly power as an instrument of God's Kingdom. They were not triumphalist; they were not empire-builders – and their buildings illustrate this. In Ireland, numbers grew so fast that massive church building was called for. They did not build large churches, with aisles, as the western Church often did. They followed the pattern of the eastern Church, which was to multiply the number of buildings, but to keep them small.

No Irish church known to have been built between the fifth and twelfth centuries is more than 60 feet long, and most are much less. The favourite number for a fellowship unit was seven small churches. The number seven was perhaps inspired by the seven churches in the Roman Province of Asia Minor, to which their beloved apostle John related.[6] There are seven such churches at Glendalough and seven at Cashel. No church is known to have existed in Ireland before the Norman Conquest that can be called a basilica (a large ornate building designed to attract one-off visitors).[7]

No empire-building

The temptation to hijack the psychic energy of God's people for empire-building instead of serving has to be resisted in every generation. Brother Roger of the present-day Taizé community was offered a house. He gave this as his reason for declining it. 'It will make everything so complicated.' Juan Ortiz, the South American pastor, was offered a range of houses for his work. However, his challenge to those who offered them to him was: 'No. You keep them, but you run them for God. He will lead you.'

There is a thin line between genuine exhortation and various forms of subtle pressure that are in truth manipulation. One form is the arousal of guilt feelings, which is justified on account of the hoped-for eternal results. All too often compliance and conformity, rather than faith, is the real prize being sought; but a true Christian spirit cannot be faked: it is not conformity; it is a freely given mutual love. It is all too easy for the hidden agenda of any Christian to be that of his own ego, disguised by pious proposals. The only true gain to the Kingdom of God is when we inspire another person to join Christ's 'pilgrimage of trust on earth'.

In post-communist eastern Europe, the mistreatment of minorities by newly dominant churches has caused disillusionment with the Church. The people conclude that the Church only opposed communist power in order to replace it with church power. Attendance at one Warsaw church has plummeted from 80 per cent to 8 per cent of the population.

The Celtic Church renounced power as a way of advancing God's Kingdom, but the love and power of God so shone through its members that the people were attracted to them. It is true that the Celtic Church has been derided for this, and the power-based Roman Church nearly managed to extinguish the Celtic way. Yet today there is the chance of a significant number of members in all the churches *choosing* voluntarily the way of vulnerability and non-manipulation, the way of the Holy Spirit. Today, even scoffers in the Church may recognise that this is in the Church's own self-interest; it is a precondition of its survival in the market-place of the modern world.

A Prayer
Lord, help us to let go of:
attitudes and practices that put barriers between
the Church and the people
clerical power and status
cultural elitism in worship and custom
treating the Church as our property
pharisaical attitudes towards non-Christians.
May the Church live again for the people, sharing their joys and
sorrows in obedience to you.

A Response
Pray for these new attitudes, and make new friends.

19

Compassion for the Poor

'The Lord lifts the poor from the dust and raises the needy from their misery' (1 Samuel 2:8).

The Celts saw Christ as the champion of the poor and down-trodden. Jesus not only 'had compassion [on the crowd] because they were like sheep without a shepherd' (Mark 6:34); he also challenged the status quo and brought good news to the section of the population known as 'the poor' (Luke 4:18). The social attitudes and structures that oppressed the poor needed to be challenged and changed, but the good news was that even within these oppressive limitations the poor could be set free from all that enslaves the spirit, and could transcend their circumstances. Jesus challenged everyone, and restored their self-respect.

Likewise, the Celtic Christian leaders challenged both rich and poor. Prayer and involvement in human needs were deeply entwined. A divorce between a personal faith and a social gospel would have been unthinkable to them. Social responsibility flowed out of a life of holiness, and required the use of the spiritual gifts.

Columba's anger was aroused when he heard of the oppression of the poor. Once, when he was staying with a poor friend, he found robbers who had royal blood carrying off his host's cattle, sheep, and even furniture. They were leaving with their third boat-load when Columba confronted them and passionately urged them to return the stolen goods. They took no notice and rowed off. So Columba prophesied: 'This miserable wretch who has despised Christ in his servants will never return to the port, for a furious storm will overwhelm them so that not one of them shall survive to tell the tale.' Alas, as with most of Columba's prophecies, this one came only too true.

Gentle Aidan kept no worldly possessions for himself. If wealthy people gave him money, then he gave it to the poor or used it to buy freedom for those who had been sold into slavery – many of whom became Christian followers. King Oswald, who invited Aidan to Northumbria, shared Aidan's heart for the poor. He was about to begin a banquet at his castle in Bamburgh when he was told that a crowd was outside begging for food. Oswald sent out the food from the table, and even had the large silver dish broken up to be shared among the poor people. Aidan was so impressed that he held up the king's right hand and asked God that it might never perish. The arm was still preserved in Bamburgh church a hundred years later, a reminder to the people of the ideal of compassion to the poor.

On one occasion, King Oswin gave Aidan a fine royal horse. But on his travels, Aidan met a poor beggar, and gave him the horse and its trappings. The king was furious, until Aidan said to him: 'Is that foal of a mare more valuable to you than the poor child of God to whom I gave it?' The king was overcome with remorse and, kneeling before Aidan, promised, 'I will never again enquire what gifts of mine you hand on to God's children.'

Christ's compassion for the poor began to be inscribed in the lives of members of the Celtic Christian communities. Their influence soon rubbed off on to the Christians who farmed the lands around, as this poem illustrates:

Remember the poor when you look out on fields you own,
　　on your plump cows grazing.

Remember the poor when you look into your barn,
　　at the abundance of your harvest.

Remember the poor when the wind howls and the rain falls,
　　as you sit warm and dry in your house.

Remember the poor when you eat fine meat and drink fine
　　ale at your fine carved table.

The cows have grass to eat, the rabbits have burrows for
　　shelter, the birds have warm nests.

But the poor have no food except what you feed them,
　　no shelter except your house when you welcome them,
　　no warmth except your glowing fire.[1]

Society changed

The hearts of the Celtic Christians went out to any distressed boy or girl: they were brought into their communities to be fed and taught. In Ultan's day, we are told there wasn't one destitute child in all Northumbria.

Brigid took action to save the lives of an entire family. The unfortunate father had, as he thought, routinely killed a fox, which in fact was the local king's pet performer! The furious king ordered that this man should be executed and his wife and children be bound over as servants. Brigid came to the rescue, and once again spiritual gifts were harnessed to social justice. In response to her outpoured prayers, a wild fox, which looked and performed tricks just like those of the king's pet fox, jumped into her chariot. Brigid went to the king to plead on behalf of the imprisoned man, explaining that it was not his fault. The stubborn king said he would only relent if he could produce another fox with the same tricks as the one that had been killed. That was the cue for Brigid to introduce her answer to prayer; her fox performed all the same tricks and amused the crowd in the same way as before. The whole court was enthralled with this sign and wonder, and the man was released. Not too long afterwards, however, the cute fox slunk away into his own freedom in the wild, never to return![2]

Once compassion for the poor became second nature to Christians, the social conditions and laws of all the Celtic lands began to be transformed. The *Senches Mor*, the great record of the Laws of Ireland, states: 'Retaliation prevailed in Ireland before Patrick, and Patrick bought forgiveness with him. So now, no one is executed for his crimes, as long as he pays *evic* – the blood fine.'

According to Gerlad, for many centuries the Welsh churches enjoyed more tranquillity than others 'for not only is protection assured for animals to pasture in churchyards, but also in boundaries far beyond'.[3] Something of this social concern was preserved in the highlands and islands through the centuries. Alexander Carmichael recounts the celebrations on St Michael's Day in nineteenth-century western Scotland: the family raise the triumph song of Michael, in praise of God who gives them food, and then go out to distribute food to the poor of the neighbourhood who have no fruits or flocks themselves. Alexander Carmichael was told:

It is proper that every husbandman in the townland should give, on the day of the St Michael Feast, a peck of meal, a quarter of struan, a quarter of lamb, a quarter of cheese, and a platter of butter to the poor and forlorn, to the despised and dejected, to the alms-deserving, and to the orphans without pith, without power, formed in the image of the Father everlasting. And the man is giving this on the beam of St Michael as an offering to the great God of the elements who gave him cattle and sheep, bread and corn, power and peace, growth and prosperity, that it may be before his abject, contrite soul when it goes thither . . . These are the people who are called 'the humane men', 'the compassionate men', and 'the good women', who are taking mercy and compassion on the poor, and on the tearful, on the dejected and the despised . . . formed in the image of the Father all-creative.[4]

A Prayer
Christ of the compassionate heart:
Today, may your mercy reach the rejected
May your mercy reach the torn
May your mercy reach the addicted
May your mercy reach the worn.

A Response
I will speak out for the poor and serve them as God directs.

20

Vocations for All

'Each one, as a good manager of God's different gifts, must use for the good of others the special gift he has received from God' (1 Peter 4:10).

Although the idea of every-member ministry is much talked about in today's Church, clericalism remains endemic. The 'shadow side' of the ordination of women to the Anglican priesthood is that women too have now become clericalised. Clergy are given an inflated idea of their calling (which actually devalues it), while many other deeply devoted Christians remain unaffirmed and unmobilised in their callings, and many talented leaders simply remain 'pew sitters' in the church. All this was not so in the Celtic Church.

For a start, the Celtic Church did not, as does the contemporary traditional Church, confuse leadership with ordination. Not all leaders were expected to be ordained, and vice versa. The natural leaders, once they became Christians, headed up the Christian mission. Columba was a giant of a leader; he was ordained a presbyter, but he never became a bishop. Once, when he discovered that a visitor to Iona happened to be a bishop, he deferred to him and asked him to preside at the Eucharist, but he never deflected his leadership of the Scottish mission on account of a bishop. As we have seen, women such as Brigid and Hilda led men as well as women, and any bishops within their orders came under their authority, but these women were not ordained.

Neither did the Celtic Church confuse vocation to a religious life with ordination. I have met all sorts of people who sensed that God wanted them to dedicate their lives exclusively and directly to his service: they were then channelled into the ordination selection system and rejected. In some cases, their lives have been shattered. James Mackey observes that Patrick

> encourages his converts to embrace the religious life as monks and nuns, or even as people simply vowed to continence . . . It seems entirely likely that these religious did not form separate communities, enclosed and living on their own, but led ascetic lives in their households. One of Iona's gifts has been to help ordinary people form a language that speaks of vocation in simple terms.[1]

In the early Irish Church, there was a 'Third Order'. In this, a Christian was not placed in a slot in an ecclesiastical organisation; he gave up private property, and so became free to let God's plan unfold. Such a Christian 'was God's man . . . to know the will of God was meat and drink, to do it was life'.[2]

Another lesson about vocation that we can learn from the Celtic Church is that there was no divorce between sacred and secular. A constant refrain in the story of Brigid is that 'she came from tending her sheep'. Even the ecclesiastical Bede could reflect upon Hilda's life in these terms: 'Her career falls into two equal parts, for she spent her first thirty-three years very nobly in the secular habit, while she dedicated an equal number of years still more nobly to the Lord in the monastic life.'[3] Bede goes on to extol the number of vocations that Hilda fostered in her monasteries, and points out that five of her pupils became bishops. Yet perhaps the most significant of all the vocations she fostered was that of the shy, illiterate herdsman, Caedmon, who became the first popular Christian songster in the English language.

Sketes (training places for the warfare of the spirit) were informal groups of cells with a small place for worship, and a rhythm of work, prayer and hospitality. The Celtic form of this, a hermitage, was often used by groups who undertook missions from such a base. Children, as well as adults, could be part of it.

The simplicity of a calling

In 1975, a number of leaders in the religious life, who had a concern to see such a new framework for vocations, met in Wales. They concluded: 'At the present time there is a remarkable revival of this form of life due to reasons which include . . . the need for highly organised Orders in the Roman and Anglican churches to recover the simplicity and humanity of its form of life in the world.'[4]

Each person has a God-given calling, a spiritual motivation. It can be lived in a framework of carpentry, computers or contemplation. God is calling some people to take vows for a period or for life; he is calling others to be publicly set aside for specific purposes, as evangelists, pastors, contemplatives, hermits, teachers, healers. He calls some to commit themselves to a particular place, to be signs of his faithfulness in a rootless generation.

A Prayer
    Call, Call, Call, great Chief of the high hills;
    Call, Call, Call, great Christ of the far paths;
    Call, Call, Call, great Counsellor of the near gate.

    Set my spirit free to soar where'ere you climb;
    Set my feet free to trek where'ere you go;
    Set my hands free to do what'ere you say.

A Response
    I resolve to find and follow my vocation.

21

One Church

'I pray that they may all be one, Father! May they be in us, just as you are in me and I am in you' (John 17:21).

In a world that is falling apart, Christians need to become a unifying force as never before. Unity is not just a pragmatic necessity; it springs from the heart of Christ. It mirrors to the world the nature of the Trinity. It is what God intends for his people.

What kind of unity did Christ envisage in this prayer of John 17:11 that was his last will and testament? Most Christians agree that there must be a common Christian doctrine. This is enshrined in the Bible, the creeds and (non-Protestants add) in the first Ecumenical Councils of the undivided Church. After that, there are two poles. One pole insists that Christ envisaged a single organisation throughout the world. This requires that there is central co-ordination of mission, ordained ministry, pastoral structures, the Christian calendar, liturgical patterns, and of the teaching of Christian doctrine and morality. The other pole insists that the only essential ingredient is the gathering of believers around word and sacrament. Is the unity Christ prayed for secured from the top down or from the bottom up, or both?

In 1992, Churches Together in England invited answers to the following question in a comprehensive five-year exercise: 'Recognising that the unity we seek is . . . rooted in the unity of God, Father, Son, and Holy Spirit . . . How should we in our generation respond to God's call to us to become one so that the world may believe in Jesus Christ?' They listed some issues on which a certain measure of agreement will be necessary for the visible unity of the Church. These included the nature of unity in: 1 the faith; 2 baptism, confirmation/church membership; 3 eucharistic communion; 4 ministry; 5 decision-making; 6 mission.

Church unity schemes and commissions have involved heroic efforts by a few, but they have sometimes lacked pulling power at the grassroots level. These efforts need to be supplemented by the fostering of an instinctive unity that frees, such as the drawing together around Celtic Christian sources of inspiration. Churches Together in Essex, for example, gather each year at the church at Bradwell founded by Cedd of Lindisfarne. Here, Anglican, Nonconformist and Roman Catholic Christians find in Cedd a brother and a spirituality with which they can identify.

So what can we learn from the Celtic Church about unity? The essence of the Celtic way of 'being church' was relationship. This relationship had three strands: 1 relationship with the Trinity, which models freedom and responsibility, the bonds of love freely given, unity in diversity; 2 relationship with fellows (Celtic churches were founded on the lines of blood kinship (clans) and of spiritual kinship); 3 relationship with those through whom Christ had handed down the Church: the apostles, Peter, John, and, nearer home, men and women such as Columba or Brigid.

Although some scholars claim that the term 'Celtic Church' is a misnomer, because churches in different kingdoms varied and were not part of one organisation, there were some vital common threads that we do well to re-examine.

The first common thread was that every Christian thought of himself or herself as part of one universal Church; secondly, they believed a common doctrine as taught by Christ's apostles. They accepted the same Bible, as approved by the one universal Church. They celebrated the same sacraments of baptism and Holy Communion (also called the Eucharist or the Sacrifice).[1] They accepted the ordination of presbyters, in a pastoral or sacramental role, as part of God's pattern for his Church; and that these were ordained by overseers, or bishops, who had been chosen to do this from among the presbyters. According to the medieval *Life of St Kentigern* by the monk Joceline, the local king and clergy elected Kentigern to be 'the shepherd and bishop of their souls' on the grounds of his Christian character and demonstration of signs and wonders. Together with a bishop who they had called over from Ireland, they consecrated him. They committed him to the Holy Spirit, 'the Sanctifyer and Distributor of all the orders, offices and dignities in the Church . . .', but they made sure they invited a bishop from Ireland to consecrate him.[2]

Members of the Celtic Church took it for granted that, when

conditions of communication made this possible, that their leaders met with leaders of the world Church, and they probably had heard that British bishops had attended the Council of Arles as early as the year 314. In their worship they drew on a reservoir that included things from the universal Church, as well as new and old local material. They celebrated the usual Christian festivals, such as Christmas and Easter; and they inherited some common practices and ideals, such as fasting, prayer and pilgrimage. And although local churches were free to take their own initiatives under the Holy Spirit, they would have been horrified at the idea of a travelling Christian starting a rival church where one already existed, as happens today. It was probably common ground that no one person's dictate should be followed without being weighed and tested -- as St Paul, in 1 Corinthians 14, urged in relation to prophecy. Above all, Christians everywhere were to model Christ's loving attitudes as described in his Sermon on the Mount.[3]

So there is little doubt that the Celtic Church accepted the principle of the universal Church, and the principle of linked oversight reflected in Christ's ordaining of apostles, and that this should be continued by their occasionally meeting together; it was accepted as natural that the leader of the Church in one of the great centres, such as Rome or Alexandria, should preside in love at synods of the world-wide Church.[4] There is equally little doubt that the members of the Celtic Church felt free to respond directly to initiatives of the Holy Spirit in evangelising, church planting and the formation of Christian communities.

The wild goose, which as we have seen is a Celtic symbol of God's Spirit, also serves as a symbol of unity. Flying alone, the wild goose can fly at less than a third of the speed that it can when it is in grouping. In formation, it can fly at about 70 miles an hour – a phenomenal speed. In the Irish Church that Patrick helped to establish, we see that Spirit-led initiatives and unity go hand in hand, with phenomenal growth as a result. The Spirit of God gave Patrick a powerful inner call to evangelise Ireland, yet he prepared for this by submitting to the training and the ordination of the wider Church.

Some noted scholars believe that Bishop Germanus of Gaul, supported by British bishops, commissioned Patrick to go to Ireland as a bishop. Yet once in Ireland, it seems that Patrick quickly discerned that each of the potential networks for Christ needed an overseer, and he himself ordained as bishops (i.e.

presbyters with responsibility for a town) many of the natural
leaders that the Christians were throwing up. The 'Catalogue of
the Saints of Ireland', which was probably written between the sixth
and ninth century, states: 'The founders of the churches were all
Bishops, three hundred and fifty in number, famed and holy and
full of the Holy Spirit. They had one head, Christ. They had one
leader, Patrick. They maintained one Eucharist, one liturgy . . .
one Easter . . . what was excommunicated by one church was
excommunicated by all.'[5]

Later, monks and other missionaries founded churches. Because
no hand of bureaucracy was being imposed, structures altered to
suit changing needs, and bishops fitted in to a monastic system
with its own natural leaders. Yet through all the change, unity and
continuity was maintained. This was perhaps the greatest period
of blessing and growth in the history of Christianity.

As the Roman Empire became disrupted, and communications
between Britain and church centres such as Rome or Byzantium
grew faint, it was natural and right that the focus of unity became
the apostles of the Christian faith in these lands. Apostles such as
David, Brigid, Columba and Aidan were themselves inspired by the
example of Christian leaders in the world-wide Church, especially
the Holy Fathers and Mothers who had followed the Spirit into
the desert as an antidote to the creeping corruption in the Church.
These British and Irish apostles passed the test of the original
Twelve. British believers could say of them, in a spiritual sense,
what was said of the Twelve in a literal sense: 'they have been with
Jesus' (Acts 4:13). Holiness shone through their lives.

Misuse of power

The problem came when the Church abroad, using worldly power,
sent new leaders who introduced customs and regulations that had
become the norm in the Empire, but that were strange to the
British, who had retained practices they believed were one with
those of the earliest Church, and who had been cut off from contact
when these had been updated on the Continent. These incoming
leaders were not perceived as 'having been with Jesus', and their
changes were not implemented in a context of fellowship.

This problem was not unique to the Celtic Church. The process
of schism between the eastern (Orthodox) and western (Roman)
Church began in 863–7 and culminated in 1054. We have to

remember that the Celtic Church drew its life as much from the eastern as from the western Church, and that most of the developments in the papacy that caused the western Church to split at the time of the sixteenth-century Reformation had not yet taken place. For example, Columbanus established so many churches in Gaul that the Celtic churches there eventually became a see under an archbishop. It was not until 1129 that Pope Innocent III pronounced that this see must be dissolved; until then, such papal claims would not have been acceptable. Nevertheless, the difficult issues were there in seed form.

The issue of whether the institutional (Roman) or the relational (Celtic) way of being Church should dominate was to come to a head. The New Testament writer of the Letter to Hebrew Christians urges his readers to 'greet all your leaders and all God's people' (Hebrews 13:24). The greeting that comes from mutual respect is another mark of catholicity, but the Roman Church began to lose sight of this when it adopted Roman power structures.

Bede's account of the negotiations between Augustine of Canterbury (who, at Pope Gregory's insistence, had travelled to Arles to be consecrated the first Archbishop of the English) and the home-grown Celtic bishops is interesting. All concerned agreed that a person through whom God worked signs and wonders, as he did through the original apostles, must be taken seriously. At their first meeting, at which Augustine proposed they adopt a joint evangelisation programme, and joint regulations for festivals, sacraments and monasteries, God restored the sight of a blind man through Augustine. This predisposed the Celtic leaders, who were unattracted by the prospect of a bureaucratic blanket being imposed that could smother the life of the Spirit, to consider reconvening for further talks.

Before these began, they prayed to be shown the mind of God on this matter of forsaking their traditions. They asked the advice of a wise and holy hermit; to them, authority lay more in such a person than in a dignitary. The hermit advised them that if Augustine was a man of God, they should follow him. They would know if he was, for if he rose to greet them, this would show that he had a Christ-like humility. Alas, pride ruled Augustine's visit, and he didn't stand up to greet them; thus the Celtic church leaders refused to follow him.

Later, at the 664 Council of Whitby, uniformity in certain

observances, such as the monastic tonsure and the date of Easter, was imposed upon the Church in Northumbria. King Oswin convened the council, which met at the Whitby monastery by invitation of Abbess Hilda, who was a friend of protagonists on both sides. The king asked the spokesmen of each side to state their case. Wilfred was brilliant, arrogant and disparaging towards those who followed the Celtic way. The king ostensibly decided in favour of Wilfred's case on the (spurious) grounds that the observances he advocated were derived from Peter, and all sides agreed that Peter's authority was greater than that of any regional church apostle. Some scholars believe that the king had made up his mind beforehand on the grounds of political expediency. Over the ensuing centuries, the churches in the rest of England, Ireland, Wales and Scotland also acquiesced in the centralised Roman practices.

Many Roman Catholics believe this measure was essential to the unity of the universal Church. 'It preserved the links', they say. There is a contrary view: that the arrogant manner of its imposition built in a hidden disunity which, surfacing at the time of the Reformation, has led to endless fragmentation.

Certainly, the fruit of the Council of Whitby was a sharp decline in spiritual quality, and therefore in the spiritual authority that is the guarantor of unity. As Magnus Magnusson tellingly puts it:

> Celtic monks lived in conspicuous poverty; Roman monks lived well. Celtic monks were unworldly, Roman monks were worldly. Celtic bishops practised humility, Roman bishops paraded pomp. Celtic bishops were ministers of their flocks, Roman bishops were monarchs of their Dioceses. Celtic clergymen said 'Do as I do', and hoped to be followed; Roman clergymen said 'Do as I say', and expected to be obeyed. Like the Roman Empire that they were wanting to re-establish throughout Europe, the mandarins of the Roman hierarchy were basically authoritarian and imperialist in their outlook; the Celtic clergy knew it, and did not like it.[6]

Paternalism breeds disunity

Following the 664 Whitby decree in Northumbria, the Celtic Church accepted Roman rule in Cumbria in 704, in Cornwall in

705, in Scotland in 717, in South Wales, Somerset and Devon in 768, and in North Wales in 777. Eventually, the Church in Ireland did too. At the Synod of Cashel in 1171, the Irish monastic episcopate was abolished and continental-style episcopacy was imposed. An Irishman who lived at that time saw with foreboding all the possibilities of future corruption that went with this demeaning approach to church unity:

> More bitter to me than Death coming between my teeth are the folk that will after me . . . The Elders who did God's will at the beginning of time were bare-haunched, scurvy, muddy: they were not stout and fat!
>
> The men of keen learning who served the King of the Sun, did not molest boys or women; their natures were pure. Scanty shirts, clumsy cloaks, hearts weary and piteous, short rough shocks of hair – and very rough monastic rules. There will come after that the Elders of the latter-day world, with plunder, with cattle, with mitres, with rings, with chessboards . . . I tell the seed of Adam the hypocrites will come, they will assume the shape of God – the slippery ones, the robbers![7]

It would be wrong, and unhistorical, to imply that Celtic and Roman Christians never worked together. Fursey, a Celt from Ireland, and Felix, a Roman priest from the Continent, evangelised East Anglia in the seventh century. They won so many people to Christ that a diocese was formed with a cathedral at Elmham. There was one diocese and one cathedral for all the churches, whether Celtic or Roman in ethos.

After the Synod of Whitby, some of the monks from Lindisfarne returned to Ireland brokenhearted, but not one set up a church in opposition. Cuthbert was made prior and abbot of Lindisfarne. Just as he had earlier fought to preserve local customs, so now he fought to preserve unity in the Church; thus he carried on a Spirit-filled ministry within the new framework. He insisted that all his monks adopt the calendar and customs decided upon at Whitby, while he continued to model the Christ-like spirituality of the Celtic mission.

The monks argued against some of the new rules, especially at having to change their varied dress for the dull uniformity of the Roman habit. When there was quarrelling at meetings, Cuthbert would walk out and resume the next day, smiling as if nothing had happened. His dying words to his brothers were to live in peace with one another, in unity with the one Church, and to practise hospitality. And on her death bed, Hilda, who hosted Whitby, and who must have been deeply disappointed at the result, pleaded with her sisters to foster peace, not only among themselves, but 'with all others'.[8]

Ireland at that time was still outside the jurisdiction of the Roman Empire. Its Church certainly believed that the authority Christ gave to his apostles had been handed on, but also that holy lives were vital if that authority was not to be undermined. That intrepid Irish missionary, Columbanus, planted so many monastic churches on the Continent that he confronted issues that those back home could evade. He had to deal with the godless character of some church leaders, yet at the same time he had to 'do business' with them in their calling as overseers of the universal Church, in order to get permissions for his developing work. His letter to Pope Boniface IV in 613, at a time when there were two power-hungry rivals for the 'Chair of Peter', is instructive:

For all we Irish, inhabitants of the world's edge, are disciples of Saints Peter and Paul and of all the disciples who wrote the sacred canon (i.e. of the New Testament) by the Holy Spirit. We accept nothing outside the evangelical and apostolic teaching. None of us was a heretic, no one a Jew, no one a schismatic; but the Catholic Faith, as it was first transmitted by you, successors of the holy apostles, is maintained unbroken. . . For among us it is not who you are but how you make your case that counts. Love for the peace of the Gospel forces me to tell all in order to shame both of you who ought to have been one choir. Another reason is my great concern for your harmony and peace. 'For if one member suffers all the members suffer with it'. As I have said before, we are bound to the Chair of St Peter. Though Rome be great and famous, she is great and renowned among us only because of that Chair. . . If it may be said that you are almost heavenly beings because of Christ's twin apostles. . . then Rome is also the head of the Churches of the world, except for the special prerogative of the place of the Lord's Resurrection. Thus, as your honour is great in proportion to the dignity of your See, you need to take equally great care not to lose your reputation through some error. Power will rest with you just so long as your principles remain sound. The real Key-bearer of the Kingdom of heaven is he who opens up true knowledge to the worthy and shuts it to the unworthy.

Therefore, my dearest friends, come to an agreement quickly . . . I can't understand how a Christian can quarrel with a Christian about the Faith. Whatever an Orthodox Christian who rightly glorifies the Lord will say, the other will answer Amen, because he also loves and believes alike. 'Let you all therefore say and think the one thing', so that both sides 'may be one' – all Christians.[9]

Unlike the Celtic Christians, we have to live with the legacy of the terrible church schisms between the eastern and western Church in the eleventh century, and between the Reformed and Roman Churches in the sixteenth century – and between a multitude of 'DIY church groups' this century. Yet we do not have to be the prisoner of history; instead, we can learn from it. If we take our cue from the Celtic bishops who learned from a holy hermit that humility and hospitality are true marks of apostolic succession, we might find the Pope, the Patriarch and the Archbishop of Canterbury conferring and praying together in a hermitage far from any of their headquarters. And they might do this regularly, building such a relationship of trust that ex-communication of the others or of their flocks becomes unthinkable. Archbishop Derek Worlock, Bishop David Sheppard and Moderator John Newton have shown the way in the partnership of trust they have created in Liverpool.

Tradition

The word 'tradition' evokes conflicting reactions among Christians. To conservative-minded church people, almost anything that has been handed down by our Christian forebears is sacrosanct, and to tamper with it is sin. For them, the attempt to disentangle the kernel from the fruit that contains it is doomed to failure: it seems like blasphemy; it indicates irreverence, foolishness and ignorance. To such people, the essence of Christianity is to be faithful to 'The Great Tradition'. One leader of an independent house church, in contrast, asserts: 'The reason the old churches are so ineffective is that they are tied to tradition. We have got rid of it and are free to respond to God in any way that seems appropriate. This freedom means we can be effective.'

No Bible-believing Christian can deny that the experience of Jesus' transfiguration (Mark 9) was connected with tradition – Moses and Elijah were the representatives of the two traditions of the Law and the prophets. For Jesus, however, it was a dynamic, living tradition. And so it was for the Celtic Church, which was like the person Jesus commended for bringing 'out of the storehouse things new and old' (Matthew 13:52).

Celtic Christians were not slaves to tradition, but they were stewards of it. They had eyes to see God everywhere – in nature, in the present situation, and also in what had been handed down to them. Patrick taught all his churches to make a cherished tradition of repeating the time-honoured words 'Mercy Lord, mercy Lord, have mercy Lord'. Yet tradition was vibrant, evolving, flexible, as we see in the change from a diocesan to a community structure in Ireland's post-Patrick Church.

Since the time of the Reformation, each side holds the other side responsible for putting certain things right: Protestants hold Roman Catholics responsible for abuses of practice and doctrine; Roman Catholics hold Protestants responsible for wilful rebellion and disunity. There is one aspect of the Reformation that each side remains responsible for: sustaining Christian relationships even in disagreement. There follows an agenda for repentance and reconciliation.

In this way, a Protestant is not dismissive of the Pope. She honours him and weighs his words seriously. By doing this, she is not giving the Pope her go-ahead to rob other members of the body of Christ of their role; he can be corrected as Paul corrected Peter; if he interferes in spheres that are not for him, she can refuse to accept such interference. Yet still she honours him. Similarly, a Roman Catholic can serve a Protestant as if she were Christ.

In his love, our God has disciplined his Church. The collapse of Christendom and the decline in the churches in Europe are but signs of this. As a result, church people in all traditions are once again needing to understand the church as *koinonia* – that giving and receiving love that permeates the life of the Trinity. This is central to the understanding of ARCIC (the Anglican–Roman Catholic International Commission).

Mary Tanner, a member of that Commission, writes:

The Church is the first part of the world drawn into the orbit of God's love – the Church is, in this sense, the world ahead of itself. If God unites, ought not the world to see in us a people in whose life the personal and relational is always prior to the institutional? Without the institutional the personal and relational is always hampered, but we cannot grow in institutional unity unless that springs out of a growth in personal communion. We must be at peace with one another; we must listen attentively to one another; we must submit to one another; we must learn to trust one another; we must love one another. These attitudes are the living tissue of our unity.

If 'God unites', ought not the world to see in us a unity which is not uniformity, but also a multiplicity which is not limitless pluralism? A diversity in which the gospel is lived in each place authentically in the bodies, skins, dances, languages and thought-forms of that place? The essence of catholicity is not the imposition of a particular limited cultural norm on everyone by some central superchurch, but the ability of each local Church to recognise and delight in every other community as an authentic form of the one universal Church. And this is why our cultural and ethnic differences are gifts God gives to us and which we are called to offer one another . . .

If we could live together in a visible unity bearing the cost of differences, never again saying to one another 'I have no need of you', we should show a model of living and loving which is grounded in that mysterious trinitarian life at whose heart is forever a cross.[10]

Alhough formal church unity schemes make chequered progress, a sea-change is taking place. 'Churches Together in Britain and Ireland' now relate to one another as 'not strangers, but pilgrims together'. In prophetic messages within all churches, God speaks not to members of a denomination, but to 'my people'. Thus God is restoring an instinctive unity to his people. Some local ecumenical partnerships, as with my own church in Bowthorpe, are truly becoming 'the Christian Church' in that locality, one family of Christians seeking to model Christ to the neighbourhood.

Now that instant communication is possible across the world, we ought to be able to look forward to the leaders of the world's main Christian streams becoming a community of trust and prayer.

Once that experience of Christian community has been established, inter-communion must be reinstated between those streams.

A growing number of Christians sense God calling them to make penance at Whitby, the place where rules were imposed but relationships were destroyed in A.D. 664. We ought to expect that the next time a Pope visits England, he will make penance at Whitby with representatives of English, Welsh, Scottish and new churches, and that the healing and renewal of Christ's body will result. For, as Dave Fitzgerald (a founder member of the band called Iona) observes, those wild geese flying in formation carry a message to us about unity: 'When Christians try to fly alone – or live in fragmented denominations – we have no power, but when we let the Holy Spirit bring us all together, it's powerful.' The Church must be visibly one, habitable, welcoming, a true reflection of God's love.

A Prayer

Lord, I am sorry for the ego trips and power-seeking, for the self-sufficiency and lack of accountability to the rest of your Body, which have so often marred the life of your Church, of which I am part.

Thrice Holy God, eternal Three-in-One,
Make your people holy, make your people one.
Stir up in us the flame that burns out pride and power;
Restore in us the love that brings the servant heart to flower.
Thrice holy God, come as the morning dew;
Hold up in us your love, which draws all lesser loves to you.

A Response

I unite myself with Christ in his word, in his sacrament, and in those in oversight in all the churches, for whom I pray.

22

'Go-with-the-flow' Evangelism

'Go then to all peoples everywhere and make them my disciples' (Matthew 28:19).

The Decade of Evangelism culminates in the 2,000th birthday of Jesus Christ. What birthday present will give him most pleasure? The 'present' proposed by one church's international evangelism director is half the world's populations acknowledging Jesus as Lord.

However, there is an enormous stumbling block. Evangelism, in Britain at least, has gained a bad name. The majority of church-goers dislike the term, cringe at the idea of evangelising, and reject it as something culturally alien.

Meanwhile, the remorseless decline in church-going continues. The Church of England's Board of Mission stated in its *Decade News*: 'Modern Britain is post-Christendom. Eighty-six per cent of children have no connection with any Christian Church during their childhood. The great Christian words like "cross" . . . "baptism" . . . even "Jesus" bring no images to many people's minds and evoke no emotion.'

The report goes on to suggest that we need a new, yet old, model of evangelism:

The last time when this land was fundamentally non-Christian was 1,400 years ago when the Anglo-Saxon pagans conquered the land. How did our forefathers cope? Can we learn from their experience of evangelising non-Christian culture? . . . For the Celts the Diocese was people – usually a tribe – and the chief evangelist was the bishop leading teams of priests and lay people. They were wanderers for the Gospel – experimenting, adventuring for the Lord . . . Evangelism sprouting from places of prayer and scholarship . . . evangelism which fits the society it addresses . . . evangelism reliant upon teams of Spirit-guided men and women . . .[1]

One thing that the Celtic churches had in common was a missionary spirit. The Celtic evangelists attracted the people to Christ by sharing their humanity with them, transfigured by Christ. They had taken on board Irenaeus' insight that 'the glory of God is seen through a human life fully lived'. They went with the flow of corporate life, too. That is why the evangelisation of the ethnic groups in seventh-century Britain had street credibility and was so successful.

Ian Bradley observes that the Celtic missionaries

adapted their methods to the social and cultural mores of the people who they were seeking to convert. Realising the power of tribal loyalty they sought first to convert kings and princes . . . in a sense they very effectively 'worked the system'. Celtic Christianity spread so rapidly through the British Isles partly because its evangelists tailored it so well to the norms and needs of . . . society . . . It was a particularly good piece of religious inculturation.[2]

The earliest evangelisation, after the departing troops of the Roman Empire left fifth-century Britain prey to plunder and chaos, came through Christians inspired by Antony and the holy men and women of the Egyptian deserts. It was said of Antony that when he died he left only two things behind: his cloak and a desert full of monks. Welsh and Cornish people who fled for their lives to the safe haven of Brittany (helping to form a largely Christian Celtic nation known as Armorica) soon wandered back and evangelised the land they had left. There were three main groups: holy people such as Illtyd and Cadoc who established monastic communities; bishops, such as David and Teilo, who led missions; and pilgrim saints and hermits. There were both men and women, and there was considerable interchange between these groups.

Natural and inspired evangelism

The life of Illtyd's disciple, Samson, furnishes us with insights into several aspects of evangelism.[3] There was evangelism through the flow of family. Samson renounced the home comforts of family in order to follow Jesus. However, when his father appeared to be terminally ill, Samson agreed to visit his family once more. The result was prayer, healing of his father, and a deep conversion of his whole family to Christ. They not only helped Samson in his outreach; they planted new churches themselves.

There was evangelism through the flow of direct inspiration. Bishop Dubricius saw God's anointing on Samson, and ordained him a bishop. To become a bishop meant he was free of organisation; he was a flying bishop, free to evangelise where the Spirit led him. How different things became later! Samson decided to journey to Brittany and found Christian communities there. En route he asked for hospitality at a monastery. Someone there had a word from God for him: 'Before you cross the Channel and reach Europe, the Lord wants to give some outward sign of his power working through you in the region you have to pass through in this country.' Samson knew it was the Holy Spirit speaking. He rearranged his plans and, with his team, his belongings, his chariot and his horses, he traversed Cornwall with the gospel.

On their way through Cornwall, Samson's team came across a band of pagans offering devotions to an idol at a place known as the Hundred of Twigg. Samson and two brothers spoke to the leader and encouraged him to give up this practice. He was unconvinced. However, God used circumstances to intervene. A boy on a horse raced by and was thrown to the ground. Everyone gathered round and there were tears for the apparently dead boy. Samson said: 'I see your idol can do nothing for this boy. If you promise to destroy this idol and cease to worship it, I will raise this boy to life with God's assistance.' The man agreed, and the boy was restored to life. As a result, the entire band of pagans gathered round, received instruction, and were baptised.

There was evangelism through signs and wonders. The Bible tells us that 'many people believed in the Lord' after Peter restored a widow to life (Acts 9:42); similarly, many of the Picts believed in the Lord after Columba restored to life the son of a Pictish chief who had been baptised with his household. As Samson stepped eshore in Brittany, he was met by a man who had a leprous wife and a demon-possessed son. He healed them both, and performed signs and wonders throughout that region; this led to the founding of the great Dol Monastery and of many other churches. This was in the context of a high level of expectation among the people. For example, the man who met Samson on the shore had been praying for help, and God had led him to expect that someone would arrive by boat who would be his agent of healing.

Not only was there evangelism through signs and wonders, but also through lasting signs marked on standing stones in key places. Samson's nephew (the author of the life of Samson) tells how Samson carved with an iron instrument the sign of the cross on an existing standing stone, and how he personally visited the large standing cross that Samson left on the top of the hill where the idol had once been worshipped. These standing stones made an immediate impact, and served as a constant reminder of Christ's sacrifice, of his teaching, or of apostles who modelled his way.

John Skinner of the Northumbria Community writes of his pilgrim travels:

> Again we were following in the footsteps of our Celtic Fathers, whose love for the Lord compelled them to take the Good News to other lands. The Celtic crosses in the market towns of both Ireland and Brittany stand as memory stones of a faith that once was ablaze with the love of God, and as waymarks, pointing us to return to the Cross, our way of Life.

Today the media serve a similar purpose to those stones, but they too often communicate a godless message. The importance of signs that stand for Christ amid modern idolatries cannot be underestimated.

In Ireland there was evangelism through 'spreading the nets wide' – that is, through working with the grain of cultural patterns. One of Ireland's earliest evangelists, Patrick, and his successors, learned the evangelistic lesson taught by the risen Christ when he told his disciples to let down their fishing net in yet another place; they put the net in the direction many fish swam in, and caught a multitude (John 21:1–14). Patrick wrote: 'It is very necessary to spread our nets, so that a copious multitude and crowd may be taken for God, and that everywhere there may be clergy, who shall baptise and exhort a people needy and anxious, as the Lord admonishes and teaches in the Gospel.'[4] It is thought that a higher percentage of the population became Christians in seventh-century Ireland than in any other country since. This was probably because a pure passion for Christ was blended with a way of being church at the centre of the natural patterns of communication, work and community.

Affirming evangelism

From Iona, Columba's Irish exiles spread Christianity to the north and west of Scotland. The Columban church sent out evangelists far and wide.

One story of Columba helps us to see the effectiveness of evangelism that goes with the flow of what is good in human nature. Columba and his team were on a journey near Loch Ness when Columba had a foresight of angels being sent to carry a man out of this world. The man was a pagan, but he had preserved the natural goodness of life even into extreme old age. Columba took this as a divine cue to hurry to this man's house at what is now Glen Urquhart, to introduce him to Christ and baptise him before he died. The outcome was that the man's son and all his household also believed and were baptised.[5] This 'pinpoint' evangelism is impossible if we are packaged and pressured, for there can be no 'seeing of angels' in such an environment. However, Christians who wait on the Lord in order to see people through whom natural goodness is flowing, as God sees them, and who go to them to affirm what is good – but also to introduce them to the One who completes and gives eternal meaning to their lives – are truly treading in the steps of Columba.

Evangelism the Aidan way

Aidan, Iona's greatest missionary, has been called 'apostle to England'. Northumbria's King Oswald had invited Iona to send a mission team to his kingdom. It failed. Its leader, Corman, branded the Northumbrians a 'rude and barbaric people', and claimed that 'no one could make it possible to turn them to a more gentle way of life'. Back at Iona, Aidan said to the mission team, 'You should first have given them the milk of milder instruction, until gradually nourished with the word of God . . . they would be able to substitute the more sublime teaching.' That was the cue to send Aidan to head up a second mission team, and to establish the famous base at Lindisfarne.

Aidan's mission to Northumbria was fruitful because he was on a level with the people, and shared their human concerns. Once he had established his missionary monastic centre, and a school for local boys whom he trained up as missionaries, the outreach began in earnest. Generally he insisted on *walking* everywhere he went.

This was surprising, because in that society the upper class rode horses; only the peasants walked, and Aidan as a bishop would have been viewed as upper class. But Aidan wanted to talk to the people, so he stopped and spoke to everyone he met in the lanes. 'Are you a Christian?', he used to ask. If the person said 'Yes', then Aidan asked them to be a better one. If the person said 'No', then Aidan said, 'May I tell you about it?' This method was successful. Aidan clearly came across to others as a genuine and approachable man. As his life and work developed, local people began to look forward to his visits. He must have tramped thousands of miles of Northumbrian lanes during his sixteen years as a bishop.

Another key to evangelism the Celtic way was the conversion of people in authority who opened doors for evangelism among their people. In this way, young men trained at Lindisfarne were able to evangelise many southern parts. The old war-like king of Mercia became a Christian two years before he died, and welcomed four priests from Lindisfarne to bring the Christian faith to those who had been their enemies. Cedd was one of these. Soon, however, Cedd was needed elsewhere.

The Northumbrian king Oswy had led his friend Sigbert, king of the East Angles, to Christ. Sigbert invited Cedd and a team to evangelise his people. As a result, they established churches and monasteries everywhere. Cedd's brother Chad made his base at Lichfield, and led evangelistic missions in that region.

Above all, it was the loving-kindness of these missionary men and women that won the hearts of the people to Christ. Bede wrote that when anyone met such a monk or priest on the road

> they ran to him and bowed, eager to be signed by his hand or receive a blessing from his lips. Whenever he spoke he was given an attentive hearing . . . When a priest visited a village, the people were quick to gather in some cottage to hear the word of life, for priests and clerics always came to a village solely to preach, baptise, visit the sick and, in short, to care for the souls of its people.[6]

Today, the average citizen regards the Church as irrelevant to his or her life, yet the clergy still behave as if most people think the Church is 'it'. Unfortunately, it isn't. What will reach the people, though, is a task force. A *Church Times* report suggests this change of gear is possible today. When 1,500 children from coalmining villages were brought to sing carols at Westminster

Abbey, conducted by their bishop, a spokesperson said: 'People were amazed that the Church should be taking their crisis so seriously. They've had to reassess their position. The church is relating to the whole spectrum . . . to show we care'; and a local secretary of the National Union of Miners said: 'There's been a definite move towards the church by the people.'[7]

> His love that burns inside me
> impels me on the road
> to seek for Christ in the stranger's face
> or feel the absence of his touch.[8]

Once, as I knelt in prayer at the foot of the statue of Aidan on the Holy Island of Lindisfarne, I was given these words:

Oh Aidan, you had the vision of a population transformed in Christ;
> You had the faith to come;
> you had the gentleness to win the hearts of king and commoner;
> you were of the people because you were of Christ;
> you patiently tended the sick and dying;
> you created teamwork;
> your visits to tell people the good news gave your team a pattern to follow;
> you loved the people of the island;
> you lived simply and prayed much.

> You prepared a mission to the Kingdom;
> you influenced others to reach yet others for Christ;
> you are Christ for this nation;
> you are apostle to this land;
> you are in pain that people here are heedless of your Lord;
> you will not rest until they are won.
Father, put the mantle of Aidan upon me.[9]

Evangelists with Celtic fire and flair planted churches across Europe in the sixth to ninth centuries, as the map on p.172 reveals. It was an astonishing achievement.

Celtic-inspired missions, Irish and English, from the sixth to the ninth centuries (approximate positions)

Working with gospel-friendly trends

The Celtic mission was successful because the Christians went with the flow of human patterns in as far as they were not intrinsically godless. Thus they used the natural networks, but confronted anti-Christian (and therefore in a sense unnatural) networks such as those of the shamans, who used spells and invoked occult powers.

Whether a people accept a faith or not can depend on the unconscious assumptions that underlie their culture. There may be attitudes and beliefs – about the universe, humankind or what makes people tick – that are so deeply ingrained as to be unquestioned. As Bishop Hugh Montefiore writes, these 'root-paradigms' of society are a very important, though usually neglected, reason for the failure of Christian mission. 'If the underlying assumptions and attitudes are not "Gospel-friendly",' he argues, 'the Gospel in that country will not prosper.'[10]

It is widely assumed that the prevailing paradigm of today's society, unlike that of Celtic times, is that life is essentially materialistic; it is therefore assumed that no amount of evangelism will turn the tide. In fact, there is a growing disillusionment with materialism, and this is expressed in a variety of ways. During a church growth workshop I asked a group to draw up a list of trends that form points of connection for today's Christian mission. They included these gospel-friendly trends:

> alternative medicine
> ecology
> animal welfare
> holistic approaches
> creative pursuits
> beauty
> healing
> peace movements
> total fitness
> meditation
> the search for identity and roots
> the search for love and belonging
> the hospice movement
> justice

New movements such as the Community of Aidan and Hilda seek to develop people-friendly models of mission that harness trends such as these to the message of the eternal Christ. Thus people who are dedicated to one of these good human concerns find that Christians stand alongside them, and that their faith enables their ideals to be lived, and to be harnessed, to the source of all that is good, and to the one who has overcome the things that destroy these ideals and prevent their fulfilment. For example, someone values the care a hospice offers to a dying relative; this leads them to value the faith that inspires Christians to cherish life and to found hospices. Through such a dynamic, our lands can be truly evangelised.

A Prayer
>Lead me, Lord, to the places in our society which are gospel-friendly:
>>May I be friends with all people
>>That they may find you as the True Friend of all;
>>May I feel the thirst of the people
>>That they may find you as the True Fount of all;
>>May I sense the drum-beats of the people
>>That they may find the drum-beats of your heart.

A Response
Inspired by the example of the New Testament and Celtic apostles in evangelism, I will seek with Christ to go with the flow of human life and bear witness wherever opportunity is given.

23

Healing of the Nations

'The leaves of the tree are for the healing of the nations' (Revelation 22:2).

In about 563, Columba was ostracised when he arrived at a church synod at Teltown, territory that was hostile to his clan. Brendan of Birr alone rose to greet him. He explained, 'I dare not slight the man ordained by God to lead nations into life.'

The concept of *nations* receiving life, or healing, is alien to individualistic Christians who have lost touch with a biblical world-view. Jesus taught us to pray 'Your kingdom come on earth', and he wept over a city and spoke prophetically to towns. God sent Jonah to save the capital city of one empire; and he sent Paul to the capital city of the Roman Empire. God gives his people a strategy for the kingdoms of this world, and he continues to send people today. The healing of ethnic groups is perhaps the greatest challenge that faces the world today.

In our pluralist society, the temptation is for the Church, as well as the world, to retreat into a ghetto mentality. Both have much to learn from the Celtic movement, which transformed bigotry and intolerance between rival ethnic groups.

David brought Christ's light to Wales at a time when the darkness of pagan invasions enveloped many other areas. Patrick, who brought Christ's light to Ireland, was sent from Britain. Columba and his men, who brought Christ's light to England, were sent from the Scottish island of Iona. David, Patrick, Columba, Aidan – each had a philosophy, a passion and a plan to enthrone Christ at the heart of the lands we now know as Wales, Ireland, Scotland and England. Cultures and kingdoms were changed.

Yet it seemed an impossible task. Tribal hostilities were entrenched by barbaric hostilities. This confronted them, as it confronts us, with the question: how can Christians who renounce power as a means even to a good end, connect with the centres of power and shape a culture for Christ?

This question confronted a group of Welsh nationalists whose fast against the British government's ban on the Welsh language I joined. As I learned of their history of oppression, I realised that the real enemy was English materialism, not the English themselves. And as I learned of their Celtic Christian birthright, I understood that the best way to overcome an evil is not to demonise other nations, but to export one's own faith to them. 'The Welsh nation retained its civilisation intact in the fifth and sixth centuries when the lights of Christianity were extinguished all over Europe. The export of Christianity to Ireland and other parts of western Europe at this time was Wales' greatest contribution to civilisation.'[1]

This question confronts Scots today who groan under the patronising incomprehension of an English-dominated government, and who find the English Church a distasteful mirror image. One Scottish church leader told me that Scotland defines itself in terms of the England it is against; but healing would be possible if penitent, unpretentious English and Scots went deep enough, to the roots of the Celtic Church, when from Scotland the barbaric English were evangelised. For it was from Iona that the monks who evangelised the English came.

Columba's Iona monks

> made a second Iona at Lindisfarne, with its church of hewn oak thatched with reeds, after Irish tradition in sign of poverty and lowliness with its famous school of art and learning . . . Their missionaries wandered on foot over middle England and along the Eastern coast, and even touched the channel in Sussex . . . For the first time, also Ireland became known to Englishmen. Fleets of ships bore students and pilgrims who forsook their native land for the sake of divine studies . . . Under the influence of these Irish teachers the spirit of racial bitterness was checked and a new intercourse sprang up between English, Picts, Britons and Irish . . . the peace of Columba, the fellowship of learning and piety, rested on the peoples.[2]

Healing lessons for Ireland's future

I visited Falls Road and the Shankill Road in Belfast when they were strewn with burned-out cars during The Troubles, and I was welcomed to a humble home in Derry (Londonderry). Joan Tapsfield was an English civil servant who had never believed the Republican criticisms of Britain's record in Ireland, until she met a Republican fighter who had been healed of his hatred, and who was committed to change rather than to destroy the English. Joan searched the records, and was horrified to learn that these criticisms were often based on fact. She sold her home and went to live in Derry to seek to make restitution. She befriended Unionists and Republicans alike, visited prisoners, and welcomed their families to her home. She says, 'To face the past is not to forgo our patriotism, but to enhance it.'[3]

The Ulster Protestants mostly came from Scotland and honoured Columba as a hero. Columba, too, was caught in a bloody conflict. He atoned for his part in it by a life of service to another race. Yet Columba was an Irishman, and a deeper appreciation of his early life in Ireland can help to heal dismissive or guilty attitudes towards the Irish.

Columba sought to wean the soul of Ireland from witchcraft to Christ:

> To all the seven kingdoms thou didst go
> With toilsome journeyings, in sore privation . . .
> Thence to the glamorous west
> Thou turnedst, where thou didst catch, forsook, the wistful
> Witchery that hath estranged the soul of Eire
> And made her heart intransigent.[4]

The work of Columba, Irishman and Scottish settler, was to bear lasting fruit in the whole of Britain too:

> The political sagacity of the Italians, aiming first at the conversion of the rulers, proved sterile and transitory, while the loving democracy and humble saintliness of the Celtic monks planted a seed destined to have more permanent growth in British soil . . . The Central value of Bede's work is . . . his revelation of the secret life that was transforming the heart of the English . . . We sons of a civilisation nominally Christian may well learn a fresh appreciation of the startling nature of the faith we profess . . . transforming a haughty and at times bloodthirsty race into the likeness of Jesus of Nazareth.[5]

Bede criticised the Celtic Church for failing to convert the Anglo-Saxons to Christ. That accusation is not entirely true, for

Cedd and Fursey converted them in East Anglia. Certainly there were phases when no evangelism took place, but this may have been because it was impossible. Recent archaeological discoveries in East Anglia have led to speculation that there was wholesale pillage. Mass murder is not a framework in which evangelism or any other human endeavour can progress.

The legends of the British warrior Arthur give a sense of his Christ-centred strategy for the nation even during the period after the Romans left when the brutal Saxons were taking over. Arthur was thwarted by quarrelling Celtic kings, yet 'he was beginning to display that rarest of qualities: a joy inspired by hardship, deepened by adversity, and exalted by tragedy'. He was given a vision for Britain: 'A land shining with goodness, where each man protects his brother's dignity, where war and want has ceased, and all races live under the same law of love and honour . . . a land bright with truth, where a man's word is his pledge . . . where the True God is worshipped and his ways acclaimed by all.'⁶ Eventually, of course, it was left to King Alfred to make peace with the subsequent pagan invaders, the Vikings. It is interesting that even at that later stage the king chose a Celtic Christian from Wales as his guide.

The biblical image of the tree of life whose leaves are for the healing of the nations reminds us that only in the Spirit of God can the wounds and divisions of peoples be healed.

Christian Ireland became a source of such healing. It was a land of continuous learning, of freedom and eloquence, of sprightliness, chattiness and spirituality. The power of Ireland has been to absorb those who come in, as well as to send out a never-ending stream of healing agents to the four corners of the world. Sometimes the healing communities founded by Irish saints, such as Columbanus' Monastery at Bobbio, in Italy, seemed to lie dormant. Then, in the midst of prevalent corruption in churches and monasteries, a Francis of Assisi could train at a place such as Bobbio, there rediscover threads such as restitution, blessing of creation and cross-shaped praying, and go out to bring a new dose of healing to the world.

The tragedy of Ireland, which is really the tragedy of Britain, is that the land of healing has become the land of division. The Unseen Doorkeeper at the Anglo-Irish Door of Destiny seeks to kindle again the flame that a Briton once brought to Ireland, and which, after it had been extinguished in Britain, the Irish brought back. As that flame burns, so a new and healing partnership of love will dawn. For the purpose of the healing of the Celtic lands is to bring healing and hope to humanity. The US chapter of the Community of Aidan and Hilda is committed to healing the wounds inflicted upon the native Indian people of America by the Europeans. Others are sowing the seeds of healing between east and west, and between the poor south and the rich north.[7]

A Prayer

Lord, I pray for the healing of Britain and Ireland
May they become lands where the true God is worshipped
and his ways acclaimed by all.
Transfigure our offices and factories, our schools and town halls,
our media and leisure,
Till they become your instruments, like fingers on a hand.

A Response

Wait on God to be shown the centres of power in your line of vision.
Pray for them and respond to what God puts into your heart.

24

Angels

'The angels . . . are spirits who serve God and are sent by him
to keep those who are to receive salvation' (Hebrews 1:14).

The now-fading age of rationalism poured scorn on the idea of
angels. Stories of angels were lumped together with fairy stories
in the popular mind, and were an embarrassment to liberal
Christians. However, two things are now beginning to dawn on
people who hold this attitude. The first is that this dismissal of a
whole area of reality has created a vacuum, a vacuum that is now
being filled by a vast industry that panders to people's fascination
with devils and the occult. The second is that the reason angels
seemed to disappear may be because Christians, like everyone
else, had lost the necessary faculty of perception.

David Adam has written:

> We are bombarded today by so much fantasy, that it is
> necessary again to take time to be aware of the realities
> that are about us. Somehow the Celtic peoples, due to their
> history, have been able to keep an awareness of the 'other'
> far more easily than most other peoples. It was expressed in a
> beautifully simple way by a woman from Kerry in the south west
> of Ireland. When she was asked where heaven was, she replied:
> 'about a foot and a half above a person'. Such an awareness has
> us always treading exciting border lands.[1]

In the Bible, angels are messengers from God, and it is not
always clear whether they are humans, spirits, or manifestations
of God himself. And it does not matter, for the modern separation
of natural from supernatural did not exist. Unlike the fanciful
portrayals of angels in medieval times, there is an earthly reality
about angelic encounters in the Bible. Four roles for angels can

be discerned: they shield (e.g. Daniel 3:28; 12:1); they reveal God's message (e.g. Matthew 1:20); they heal (Tobit 3:17, in the Apocrypha); and they escort souls at death (Luke 16:22). Jesus taught that every child has a guardian angel (Matthew 18:10).

Experience of angels today is more common than is generally admitted. Hope Macdonald's marriage was saved when she and her husband, in a last-ditch meeting before separation, knelt at separate ends of the bed. They each independently saw a being radiant with love and light. This transformed them, and they knew they would stay together for life. As a result of this experience, Hope Macdonald began to record other people's encounters with angels. She found at least one person in every group she interviewed who had an angel experience.[2] In the United States, 'the work of God's secret agents is so well documented that bookstores have had to start special angel sections', writes Dermot Purgavie.[3]

Hope Macdonald says:

As the popularity of the occult has increased, our eyes have been blinded to the great biblical truth of the reality of God's angels . . . We must get our eyes off the devil and turn them back to the great supernatural God of the Bible. God's ministering angels are at work in the world today. Angels are created, spiritual beings; their purpose is to worship, serve, and represent God, but they cannot be everywhere at once . . . The angels protected Jesus when he was a baby. They strengthened him at his hour of temptation. They ministered to him in the garden . . . The angels rolled the stone away from the garden tomb and announced his resurrection.

The early life of Patrick written by Muirchu incorporates a tradition that 'the angel was wont to come to him on every seventh day of the week; and as one man talks with another, so Patrick enjoyed the angel's conversation'.[4] One-third of Adamnan's biography of Columba recounts his experiences of angels, and Bede's *History* frequently alludes to angel experiences.

Columba was no stranger to visits from angels, and was often aware of their comings and goings, especially to protect someone in danger or to escort a departing soul heavenward, even when these occurrences were at a distance. He speaks of them seldom, but was often in the company of angels as he prayed. One day, on Iona, he commanded his brothers to let him go alone to the

Machair, the western plain. There on a little hill he was met by many angels who were clothed in white and flew at great speed. We know this because one disobedient monk spied on the meeting and thereby cut it short. The site of this story is still recognisable on Iona.

When Cuthbert's diseased knee was badly swollen, someone on a horse rode up and said: 'Boil some wheat flour in milk, and bathe the tumour with it hot, and you will be healed'. Bede informs us:

> He mounted and rode off. Cuthbert did as he was asked and within a few days all was well again. Then he knew that it was an angel that had given him the remedy, sent by the same power who had sent the Archangel Raphael to cure Tobias' eye. If anyone thinks it is strange for an angel to appear on horseback let him read the history of the Maccabees, where angels on horseback came to defend both Judas Maccabeus and the temple itself.[5]

The archangel in Scotland

The prayers and memories recorded in the *Carmina Gadelica* by Alexander Carmichael reveal the important place angels held in the hearts of the peoples of the Scottish highlands and islands as late as the last century:

> Thou Michael the victorious,
> I make my circuit under thy shield,
> Thou Michael of the white steed,
> And of the brilliant blades,
> Conqueror of the dragon.
> Be thou at my back,
> Thou ranger of the heavens,
> Thou warrior of the King of all,
> O Michael the victorious,
> My pride and my guide,
> O Michael the victorious,
> The glory of mine eye.
>
> I make my circuit
> In the fellowship of my saint,
> On the machair, on the meadow,

On the cold leathery hill;
Though I should travel the ocean
And the hard globe of the world
No harm could ever befall me
'Neath the shelter of thy shield;
O Michael the victorious,
Jewel of my heart,
O Michael the victorious,
God's shepherd thou art.[6]

St Michael is the Neptune of the Gael. He is the patron of the sea, and of maritime lands, of boats and boatmen, of horses and horsemen throughout the West. As patron saint of the sea St Michael had temples dedicated to him round the coast wherever Celts were situated. Examples of these are Mount St. Michael in Brittany and in Cornwall, and Aird Michael in South and in North Uist, and elsewhere.

On 29th of September a festival in honour of St. Michael is held throughout the Western Coasts and Isles. This is much the most imposing pageant and much the most popular demonstration of the Celtic year. To the young the Day is a day of promise, to the old a day of fulfilment, to the aged a day of retrospect . . .

On the eve of St Michael the people bring in the carrots, kill the lamb, take each other's horses. On the Day they go to Communion, eat the lamb, circle the burial ground in pilgrimage, compete in athletics and horse racing, and distribute the carrots to those in need.[7]

I see the first rays of sunlight shimmering through a silver maple tree. I stand gazing as one in the midst of a vision . . . and then in a twinkling I'm certain. I am standing before a tree full of angels dazzling me with their glorious presence. Bright wings of fire all aglow! Such beauty! Celestial bodies trembling in the trees. Trembling in awe over the beauty of the world that I take for granted (Macrina Niederkehr, *A Tree Full of Angels*).

A Prayer
Have mercy on the little ones abused;
Tender angels draw them to your Presence,
Have mercy on those in black trial;
Singing angels lift them into your Presence,
Have mercy on the souls at death's portal;
Holy angels escort them to your presence.[8]

A Response
I will live this life in the light of eternity, and of the whole company of heaven.

25

Triumphant Dying

'Now let your servant depart in peace' (Luke 2:29).

Life is a journey from the womb to the tomb, and we should prepare
for our departure. Death is a taboo subject today. Many people die
in a hospital, but hospital staff do not prepare people spiritually for
death. Some are too fearful or thoughtless to think about it, but
God calls all Christians to live and to die well. The Celtic saints
offer us an inspiration.

The Rule of Columba urged each member to prepare for his
death. One way Celtic Christians prepared for their final death
was to regularly undergo 'little deaths'. In Advent and Lent,
for example, they would voluntarily accept the loss of earthly
comforts to which they were attached. Others embraced what
they called 'white martyrdom'. They were inspired by stories of
the heroic deaths, in the earlier centuries of persecution, of famous
Christians. This kind of physical death for Christ was known as
'red martyrdom'. Desiring to follow Christ in a trust just as total
as these heroes, Celtic Christians chose voluntarily to leave behind
everything they held most dear – home, family, security – and go
into exile for the rest of their lives for the Lord's sake. These were
the 'wanderers for the love of God'. We may be in one place, but
our inner life can always travel with God. Each day God gives us
is an opportunity for his life to shine through us, however faulty
our brain or body may be.

Another way in which these Christians prepared for their death
was to pray about it. Columba, Cuthbert, Brendan and others were
all given prophecies about the time and manner of their death.

Death need not be feared. Drythelm lived in Northumbria with
his wife, and had a near-death experience that changed his life.
Some time after he had apparently died, he suddenly sat up and the

mourners fled in panic. He, however, went into the village church
and prayed there until midnight. He then provided for his family
and went to live as a monk at Melrose. The reason for his radical
change of life was his near-death experience. Accompanied by a
radiant guide, he had been shown people in torment, alternating
between terrible heat and terrible cold. He understood that this
was purgatory; others were in paradise. He was only allowed a
glimpse of heaven; he did not go into it. At Melrose, Drythelm
often stood in the cold waters of the River Tweed and recited
psalms, even when there was floating ice! It is one of the earliest
statements of the variety of life beyond the grave to be known in
Britain. He eventually died in the year 700.[1]

We have so much to learn from our Celtic forebears about how
to prepare for death and celebrate it. The Irish still have wakes,
but the English remain stony in the presence of death. I hope
something of the spirit of triumphant dying seen in the lives of these
Celtic saints will one day touch every home and neighbourhood in
the land.

On the thirtieth anniversary of Columba's arrival at Iona, he
was suddenly tranfused into a radiance of joy. Just as suddenly, he became grey and cast down. Two friends who observed
him eventually drew out the reason for this strange experience.
Columba had earnestly prayed that he might depart into the
next life on the thirtieth anniversary of his coming. Seeing some
angels coming to welcome him to heaven on this anniversary,
he thought his prayers had been answered. But many other
churches had been praying he would live longer, and their prayers
too were heard! The approaching angels suddenly stopped, and
stood on a rock at the edge of the island. Columba told his two
friends: 'As a result of the prayers of these friends, though it
is against my dearest wish, the Lord has given me another
four years of life. When they are completed I shall pass away
suddenly without any physical illness, and depart with joy to
the Lord.'

Four years later, Columba did precisely that, but not without
choosing the moment and the manner of his going. He waited until
the festivities of Easter were over, for he did not want his death to
detract from them. In May he toured the island in a cart, spoke
to the workers on the land, and blessed the island. That blessing
had special power, and it was said no poisonous snake harmed
anyone again. On Saturday, six days later, he visited the barn and

thanked God there was plenty of grain for all his monks. He told his attendant, Diormit:

'This day is called the Sabbath, which means rest. It is indeed a Sabbath for me, for it is the last day of my life. After midnight, when the Lord's Day begins, I shall go the way of our fathers.'

On the way back Columba sat to rest. Their white pack-horse came to him, sensing his master was about to leave this earth, laid his head on Columba's chest, and made loud cries of grief. Columba ascended the hill and gave a prophetic blessing over the monastery. He returned to the monastery and transcribed, as was his custom, some more verses from the psalter. The last verse he completed was Psalm 34 verse 9: 'They who seek the Lord shall lack no good thing.' He gave final words to his brothers, and remained some hours in silence. As soon as the bell tolled for midnight, in a last burst of energy he ran into the church before anyone else had put the lights on. The church was bathed in a heavenly light.

He knelt by the altar. Diormit raised Columba's hand. He died blessing the brothers. Their faces were full of grief: Columba's face was transfixed with joy.[2]

Aidan emulated Columba's desire to die in church. When Aidan became ill near the church in Bamburgh, the monks who were with him set up a shelter there. He died standing in the presence of God and of his beloved friends. He was actually leaning against a wooden beam when he died; that beam survived two fires that destroyed the church, and people say it can still be seen in Bamburgh church today.

On the night of Aidan's death, a youth tending sheep on the hills near Melrose suddenly saw a long stream of light breaking through the darkness of the night, and choirs of angels descending to earth. They were taking a human soul of marvellous brightness to heaven. The youth, Cuthbert, was deeply impressed. The next day, influenced by the vision, he asked to become a monk at the monastery, where he was told his vision was of Aidan's death.

When Cuthbert was near to death, he chose a monk who suffered from diarrhoea to serve in his room. 'I have some marvellous news for you', the monk told a colleague on his return, 'from the moment I touched him I felt my old complaint go. Doubtless this is the action of heaven's grace, that he that had previously healed so many when strong and well himself should now be able to cure me when he is at death's door! This is a clear sign that bodily weakness is powerless to impair the spiritual force of this holy man.'3

Hilda, whose life as Abbess of Whitby, Bede observed, had 'filled all the land of Britain with the beauty of its radiance', was afflicted with debilitating fever for six years before she died. Yet she never ceased to give thanks to the Lord in public and private. On her last day she received Holy Communion, exhorted her sisters, and went joyfully to her Lord. In a monastery 13 miles away, a nun was awoken from sleep by the sound of a bell that they tolled when someone had died. She saw a vision of light streaming down from heaven into a monastery whose roof had been removed. In the midst of this light was the soul of Hilda, escorted by angels. The nun roused her sisters who spent the rest of the night in prayer and praise for Hilda. At dawn, brothers arrived to announce Hilda's death.

Bede comments: 'By a beautiful conjunction of events God arranged it that while some witnessed Hilda's departure from this life, others witnessed her entry into the everlasting life of the spirit.'4

The life of Caedmon, the uneducated farm labourer who Hilda brought into her monastery as a song-writer, came 'to a beautiful end', Bede tells us. Nearby there was a house of rest specially prepared for those near to death. People were surprised when Caedmon asked to go there, since he could walk and was chirpy. But God had shown Caedmon he had not long left on earth. On Caedmon's first day in this house, he joked with every occupant and helper until midnight. Then Caedmon asked if they had the sacrament in the house. 'Why now?' the helpers replied, 'you are not going to die yet, you seem to be in good health and spirits.' However, Caedmon took the bread of eternal life in his hand, he asked if everyone's heart was at peace with his, and quite free from anger, and told them, 'My heart is at peace, little children, with all God's servants'. Caedmon asked how long it would be before the brothers began to sing their night praises, and was told it would not be long. 'Good', he said, 'then let us wait for that hour'. He signed himself with the cross, lay on the pillow, slept for a while, and ended his life in the gentle silence.

Bede, who wrote the story of Cuthbert, Hilda and Caedmon at the monastery in Jarrow, was working on the last chapter of a book while on his deathbed. He was so weak that a young monk had to write down the words as he dictated them. The lad, Wilbert, told him: 'Dear Master, there is one sentence still unfinished'. When

Wilbert had completed the sentence, he said, 'now it is finished'. 'You have spoken truly', replied Bede, 'it is well finished'. And so he died.

To these holy friends of God there was a right moment and a right way to die, and also the right place to be buried. This was called the place of resurrection. It is possible that underlying this idea was the intuition that the Christian's work of prayer continued after death, and was particularly focused upon the place that had been God's home for them.

Brendan, who founded the large monastery at Clonfert, drew near to death at the age of ninety-three while he was on a visit to his sister, Brig. He received the body and blood of Christ. Then he told them, 'God is calling me to the eternal kingdom; and my body must be taken to Clonfert, for there will be an abundance of angels there, and there will be my resurrection.' When he had finished saying all this, he blessed the brothers and Brig. When he reached the threshold of the church, he said, 'into your hands, Lord'. Then he sent forth his spirit.[5]

We should not be misled into thinking that holiness routinely brought rosiness. Some monasteries were wiped out by plague, certain saints died in excruciating pain, others in battle, yet the note of victory was rarely absent. The young King Oswald lost his Christian kingdom as well as his life in a bloody battle, yet his dying words were a prayer for his soldiers: 'My God, have mercy on their souls'.

Columba taught Christians to treat the dead as if they were their special friends. Why? Is it because in Christ death is not an enemy of friendship, and instead it blesses it? In our superficial and mobile age we seldom stay long enough in one place to allow friendships to deepen and ripen in the way they could in the communities of Columba and Hilda. Friendships need time and rhythm. Yet as we begin to re-order our lives around a common rhythm of prayer, we find that friendships with Christians in heaven do indeed grow, and these inform and enrich our friendships on earth.

The last words and actions of great men of God in the Bible, such as Jacob (who became Israel), were understood to be supremely important. The blessings that the dying Jacob gave to his children repay study (Genesis 49). The last words and actions of Celtic Fathers and Mothers in the faith were also understood to be important.

Crowds came to hear David preach at the last Eucharist before he died. The words of his final blessing were: 'Be joyful and keep your faith, and perform the small things that you have seen and heard from me, and I will go to the road which our fathers have travelled. Be courageous whilst you are on earth, for you will not any more see me in this world.'

We not only need to forgive, release and bless others before we die, we need others to bless us. Customs chronicled by Alexander Carmichael in the *Carmina Gadelica* are well suited for adaption by today's society, and are included in a Community of Aidan and Hilda leaflet called *Preparing a Good Death*.[6] In the Scottish highlands and islands, blessings were often said over a dying person by a relative or soul friend, along with others. These death blessings are sometimes known as 'soul leading' or 'soul peace'. The soul peace should be said slowly, with all present joining the dying person in asking the Three Persons of the Trinity and the saints in heaven to receive the departing soul. During the prayer the soul friend makes the sign of the cross on the dying person's forehead or lips. Even with people with little religious background, a well-known Bible passage, hymn or one of these prayers may be a help, and a cross may be held in front of them:

Death with oil,	Death without pain
Death with joy,	Death without fear,
Death with light,	Death without death,
Death with gladness,	Death without horror,
Death with penitence	Death without grieving.

May the seven angels of the Holy Spirit
    And the two guardian angels
Shield me this night and every night
    Till Light and dawn shall come.[7]

Saviour and Friend, how wonderful art Thou,
My companion upon the changeful way,
The comforter of its weariness,
My guide to the Eternal Town,
The welcome at its gate.[8]

We will have good weather after the final raindrop.[9]

Death is going backstage to meet the author who has written his lines into every leaf and plant.[10]

A Prayer

I am going home with You, to your home, to your home;
I am going home with You, to your home of mercy.
I am going home with You, to your home, to your home;
I am going home with You, to the Lord of blessings.

A Response

Practise offering your own death as a sacrifice to God, placing
into his hands all that you have, are or ever will be; all whom you
have ever wronged, all who have wronged you. Ask the Saviour
to forgive and release them, to forgive and release you, that if
he should take you tonight, you will be one with yourself, and
one with him.

Appendix: The Way of Life of the Community of Aidan and Hilda

'For the healing of the land through men, women and children who draw inspiration from the Celtic saints'

Introduction

The Community of Aidan and Hilda is a body of Christians who wish to live wholeheartedly as disciples of Jesus Christ, and to express this in a distinctive way that draws inspiration from the lives of St Aidan and other Celtic saints. Members of the Community share the belief that God is once again calling us to the quality of life and commitment that was revealed in the lives of these Christians whose witness was so effective.

General

In common with many communities within Christianity, we have three vows. These are SIMPLICITY, CHASTITY and OBEDIENCE, which we understand as principles, not rules.

SIMPLICITY means the willingness to be poor or rich for God according to his direction. We resist the temptations to be greedy or possessive, and we will not manipulate people or creation for our own ends. We are bold to use all we have for God without fear of possible poverty.

CHASTITY means accepting and giving to God our whole being including our sexuality. We love all people as Christ commands, but the specific emotions and intimacy of sexual relations are expressed only in married life. Some will be given a gift of marriage, some a gift of celibacy, and some will be given grace to continue a journey of not yet knowing. Each is to be equally respected and rejoiced in. We respect every person as belonging to God, and we are available to them with generosity and openness.

OBEDIENCE is the joyful abandonment of ourselves to God. The root of obedience is in attentive listening to God, because the longing of our hearts is to obey him. We honour those whom God has placed in authority over us, and we seek to recognise and respect the gifts, roles and authority of those who work alongside us in the community of the Church.

Specific

The Soul Friend: The Celtic Church affirmed and used the ministry of the *anamchara* or 'Soul Friend'. A Soul Friend needs to be a mature Christian who is in sympathy with the aims of the Community. (S)he does not need to belong to the Community of Aidan and Hilda, but it is clearly helpful if they do.

Each member of this Community will have a Soul Friend to work with them in developing a Way of life that is personally suited to them. The Way relates to the following ten areas of life, and is reviewed at agreed intervals.

1 Study and Application of the Celtic Christian Way

Daily Bible reading is at the heart of this way of life. In addition, we study the history of the Celtic Church, becoming familiar with such saints as Aidan, Brigid, Caedmon, Columba, Cuthbert, David, Hilda, Illtyd, Ninian, Oswald and Patrick. We remember their feast days and consider them as companions on our journeys of faith. We also bear in mind their strong link with the Desert Fathers and the Eastern Church, and wish to draw them too into our field of studies. It is essential that study is not understood merely as an academic exercise. All that we learn is not for the sake of study itself, but in order that what we learn should be lived. We encourage the Celtic practice of memorising Scriptures, and learning through the use of creative arts.

2 Spiritual Journey

A Soul Friend is a friend with whom we openly share our spiritual journey. We meet with our Soul Friend at least twice a year. (S)he is someone who is familiar with the Order of Aidan and Hilda and who seeks to discern with us where we are on that journey, what the Spirit is doing in our lives, and how God is leading us. The Soul Friend respects the tradition that we come from. Thus, for example, some will seek a Soul Friend who is familiar with formal confession and penance.

The Soul Friend gives guidance on two disciplines that the Order considers to be important:

(1) Regular retreats. The outworking of this depends on the individual's own lifestyle, but we encourage regular days of quiet and reflection, and also an annual retreat.

(2) Pilgrimage. The purpose of pilgrimage is to tread in the shoes of Christ or his saints in order to make contact with the many rich experiences which are to do with being a pilgrim. Such pilgrimages draw us into deeper devotion to our Lord Jesus and will inspire us to mission. Members might seek out communities of prayer. The Community recommends pilgrimage to sites of the Celtic Christian tradition, such as Iona and Lindisfarne, as well as to new 'places of resurrection'. Soul Friends give guidance about different ways of making pilgrimage.

3 A Daily Rhythm of Prayer, Work and Rest
Prayer. We commit ourselves to a regular discipline of prayer. If required, our Soul Friend can give us guidance about this. The Community recommends the use of daily patterns of worship. The St Aidan Trust provides patterns of worship which are suited to the Way.

Ways of praying will vary according to temperament. The Community encourages a renewal of 'all kinds of praying' (Ephesians 6:8), and we are therefore committed to discovering new ways of praying, from contemplative prayer to celebratory praise.

Work. We welcome work as a gift from God. Every member should engage in work, whether it be the routine activities of life or paid employment. Work motivated by values which conflict with the Way should be avoided as much as possible. In humility we accept what God gives us. If we have no employment and are not clear what our work is, then we seek the advice of our Soul Friend. We seek not to overwork, standing firm against all pressure to do so, because it robs ourselves, others or God of the time we should give to them.

Rest. The hours of rest and recreation are as valuable as the hours of prayer and work. The Lord Jesus reminds us that 'the Sabbath was made for humankind, and not humankind for the Sabbath' (Mark 2:27). In the Scriptures, even the land was given a Sabbath in the seventh year (Leviticus 25:3–5). The need for rest was built into creation (Genesis 2:1–3). A provision for this kind of rest, which is both holy and creative, should be part of each member's personal Way of Life.

4 Intercessory Prayer

The Community affirms a world-view that recognises the reality of the supernatural and of spiritual warfare. As Cuthbert and others 'stormed the gates of heaven', so we also need to engage in and to become familiar with intercessory prayer. We do not project on to the supernatural what belongs to the sphere of human responsibility. We affirm national initiatives in intercessory prayer.

5 Simplicity of Lifestyle

We wish to 'live simply that others may simply live', to avoid any sense of judging one another; and God will make different demands of each of us. Our common responsibility is to regularly hold before God (and, as appropriate, to share with our Soul Friend) our income, our savings, our possessions, conscious that we are stewards, not possessors of these things, and making them available to him as he requires.

A simple lifestyle means setting everything in the simple beauty of creation. Our belongings, activities and relationships are ordered in a way that liberates the spirit; we cut out those things that overload or clutter the spirit.

We are not seeking a life of denial for we thoroughly rejoice in the good things God gives us. Our clothes and furniture should reflect God-given features of our personalities. There is a time to feast and celebrate as well as to fast. Our commitment is to openness. We stand against the influence of the god of mammon in our society by our lifestyle, by our hospitality, by our intercession, and by regular and generous giving.

6 Care for and Affirmation of Creation

We affirm God's creation as essentially good, but spoilt by the effects of human sin and satanic evil. We therefore respect nature and are committed to seeing it cared for and restored. We aim to be ecologically aware, to pray for God's creation and all his creatures, and to stand against all that would seek to violate or destroy them. We look upon creation as a sacrament, reflecting the glory of God, and seek to meet God through his creation, to bless it, and to celebrate it.

7 Wholeness, not Fragmentation
We renounce the spirit of self-sufficient autonomy, and are committed to a much more holistic approach which was the strength of the Celtic Church. We encourage the ministry of Christian healing. We not only lay hands on the sick and pray for their healing, we also 'lay hands' on every part of God's world to bless it and recognise its right to wholeness in Christ. We seek to become more fully human as we grow in Christ, and we believe that 'the glory of God is seen through a life fully lived' (Irenaeus).

8 Openness to the Wind of the Spirit
We allow God to take us where the Spirit wills, whether by gentle breeze or wild wind. The Celtic Christians had such faith in the leading of the Spirit that they gladly put to sea in small coracles, and went where the wind took them. We desire this kind of openness to the leading of the Spirit.

Essential to this is a proper affirmation of the gift of prophecy. St Paul urges us all to prophesy (1 Corinthians 14:1). We honour this gift and encourage its proper and appropriate use.

Learning to listen is a skill that has almost been lost, and which takes many years to acquire. We seek to cultivate an interior silence that recognises and sets aside discordant voices, to respond to unexpected or disturbing promptings of God, to widen our horizons, to develop 'the eye of the eagle' and see and hear God through his creation.

9 Unity and Community
As we study the history of the Celtic Church we discover the unity we once had as one Christian people within the one universal Church. We are constantly ashamed of our divisions, and we repent of the schisms that have occurred from the Reformation onwards. We look upon all fellow Christians not as 'strangers but pilgrims together', and we honour those in oversight in all

denominations. We resist all gossip and destructive talk about our own denomination or others. We resist in our own lives things that damage the unity of Christ's body, and will not do separately what is best done together.

The Celtic Church was thoroughly indigenous to the people in a way that the Church has never been since. Aidan lived alongside the people and refused to accept practices and customs that would distance him from the people and make him seem superior. The Celtic Church honoured, trusted and went with the grain of the human communities it worked amongst. We seek to cultivate a solidarity with all people in everything except sin, to value all that is truly human in them, and to shed attitudes and practices that put up barriers between the Church and the people.

We desire the healing of peoples divided by class, colour or creed and repent of our own part in these divisions.

10 Mission

Our aim is that 'the whole created order may be reconciled to God through Christ' (Colossians 1:20). We seek to live as one Christian community so 'that the world may believe' (John 17:21). The goal of the Way of Life is to develop a disciplined spirituality that will make us effective in our witness to Christ in the world.

The Celtic Church evangelised from grassroots communities such as Lindisfarne, Iona and St David's. Our evangelism springs naturally from the community of our local church, and out of the community of this order. Bishops like Chad and Cedd were irrepressible evangelists as they travelled around. As we live out this life, the Holy Spirit leads us into new initiatives to bring God to the people. These will usually be through our churches at local or wider levels. Sometimes it may be appropriate to form a mission task group with other members of the Community to pray, study and accomplish a particular God-given task.

We seek to share our faith wherever opportunity is given. We evangelise not simply out of a sense of duty, but because the Spirit of God is giving us a heart for the lost. We ask God to work through us in signs and wonders for his glory, not ours.

Our mission also includes speaking out for the poor, the power-less and those unjustly treated in our society, and to minister to and with them as God directs.

As our gifting and opportunity permit we counter all false, materialistic, New Age or occult teachings through love, sound argument, prayer and demonstrations of the power of God, in the spirit of St Patrick's Breastplate.

Celtic evangelists worked hand in hand with those in authority to bring regions and kingdoms under the rule of God, and to open the doors to the gospel. We seek to dialogue and work with people of good will in places of authority and influence so that our lands may be led by people who are led by God, and become healed lands of the glorious Trinity.

For full details or a catalogue of publications write to C.A.H., Redhill Fauni, Snitterfield, Stratford-upon-Avon, Warwickshire, CV 37 OPQ.

Notes

Part One: Roots for a Culture Change

1 The Call of Aidan Today

1 Biblical quotations unless otherwise stated are from the Good News Bible, HarperCollins.
2 Ray Simpson, *Rural Evangelism*, Epworth Press, 1975.
3 Ray Simpson, *Bowthorpe. A Community's Beginnings*, Open Door Publications, 1985; and Ray Simpson, *How We Grew a Local Ecumenical Project*, Grove Books, 1984.

2 Culture Change

1 Graham Cray, *The Gospel and Tomorrow's Culture*, CPAS, 1994.
2 George Steiner, *Real Presences*, Faber, 1989.
3 Carl Jung, *Modern Man in Search of a Soul*, Routledge & Kegan Paul, 1978.

Part Two: Lindisfarne Landmarks

1 John and the Eastern Connection

1 Bede, 'Life of Cuthbert', in *The Age of Bede*, Penguin Classics, 1983, p. 54.
2 John Scotus Eriugena, *The Voice of the Eagle*, Floris Books, 1990.
3 Lightfoot, *Apostolic Fathers*, II, iii, pp. 363–401.
4 Irenaeus, *The Demonstration of the Apostolic Preaching*, 6.
5 Ibid.
6 See Myles Dillon and Nora Chadwick, 'The Celtic Realms' (chapter 8), in *The History of Civilisation*, Weidenfeld & Nicolson, 1967.
7 Shafiq Abou Zayd Ihidayutha, *A Study of the Life of Singleness in the Syrian Orient*, OUP, 1993, quoted in A. M. Allchin, *Celtic Christianity: Fact or Fantasy?*, Allchin, 1993.
8 Quoted in Ian Bradley, *The Celtic Way*, DLT, 1993, p. 10.
9 Nora Chadwick, *The Age of the Saints in the Early Celtic Church*, OUP, 1961, p. 50.

2 Communities of Faith

1 Dietrich Bonhoeffer, *The Cost of Discipleship*, SCM, 1964, p. 107.
2 Geoffrey Ashe, *King Arthur's Avalon*, Collins, 1990, p. 55.
3 Ailred, 'The Life of St Ninian', in *Two Celtic Saints*, Llanerch, 1989.
4 Thomas Taylor (ed.), *The Life of Samson of Dol*, Llanerch, 1991.
5 Robert Van der Weyer, *Celtic Fire*, DLT, 1990.
6 Vida D. Skudder, Introduction to Bede's *Ecclesiastical History of the English Nation*, Everyman, 1930.
7 The Community of the Servants of the Will of God, Crawley Down, Sussex.
8 Father Gregory, 18 August 1993, sermon.
9 Jean Vanier, *Community and Growth*, DLT, 1979, p. 1.

3 People on the Move for God

1 *The Anglo-Saxon Chronicle, 888–900.*
2 Shirley Toulson, *The Celtic Alternative*, Random Century, 1987.
3 'The real founder of the English missionary movement on the continent was St Willibrord, who, as a young monk being trained in Ireland, absorbed not only more learning but also a stronger desire for "pilgrimage for the love of God". This desire . . . had already changed Europe'. (David L. Edwards in *Christian England Vol. 1*, Fount, 1982.)
4 Nora Chadwick, *The Age of the Saints in the Early Celtic Church*, OUP, 1961.
5 Ibid.
6 *The Voyage of St Brendan*, Floris Books, 1991.
7 Alexander Carmichael, *Carmina Gadelica*, Floris Books, 1992.
8 Ibid.
9 Alistair MacLean, *Hebridean Altars*, W. & R. Chambers, 1937, quoted in Martin Reith, *God in Our Midst*, SPCK, 1989.
10 Edward Sellner, *Soul-making: The Telling of a Spiritual Journey*, Twentythird Publications, Connecticut, 1991.
11 Glyn Brangwyn, Norwich, 4 November 1994.

4 Contemplative Prayer

1 Madeleine L'Engle, *Walking on Water*, Crosswicks, 1980.
2 Larry Dossey, *Healing Words: The Power of Prayer and the Practice of Medicine*, HarperCollins, San Francisco, 1993.
3 John Cassian, *Conferences X 7*, quoted in A. Carthusian, *The Way of Silent Love*, DLT, 1993, p. 15.
4 Quoted in Marcel Driot, *Fathers of the Desert*, St Paul Publications, 1992, p. 63.
5 John Cassian, *Conferences IX 25*.
6 Patrick, *Confession 16, 25*. See Ian Macdonald (ed.), *Saint Patrick*, Floris Books, 1992.
7 Adamnan, *Life of Saint Columba*, Llanerch, 1988.
8 Bede, 'Life of Cuthbert', in *The Age of Bede*, Penguin Classics, 1983, p. 65.
9 Nora Chadwick, *The Celts*, Penguin, 1991.

10 Echoes a prayer of Columba.

5 Rhythm in Work and Worship
1 McNeill/Troupe
2 David Adam, *Borderlands*, SPCK, 1991.
3 Whitley Stokes, *Thesaurus Palaeohibernicus: A Collection of Old Irish Glosses*.
4 Bede, *Ecclesiastical History of the English People*, Penguin, 1989, II. p. 2.
5 Leslie Hardinge, *The Celtic Church in Britain*, SPCK, 1973, chapter 4: Divine Service.
6 Thomas Taylor (ed.), *The Life of Samson of Dol*, Llanerch, 1991.
7 F. E. Warren, *The Liturgy and Ritual of the Celtic Church*, Boydell, 1987, p. 10.
8 *News of Liturgy*, Grove Books, June 1994.
9 Warren, op. cit. Jane Stevenson's weighty Introduction, p. x.
10 Ibid.
11 The Second Letter to the People of God. Taizé. Written Calcutta-Chittagong 1 December 1976.
12 *A Celtic Eucharist*, Community of Aidan and Hilda.
13 *A Pattern of Worship for St Aidan's Day*, Community of Aidan and Hilda.

6 Holy Places: Healed Land
1 Patrick Thomas, *Candle in the Darkness*, Gomer Press, 1993.
2 Paul Tournier, *A Place for You*, Highland, 1984.
3 Lewis Mumford, *The City in History*, Penguin, 1991.
4 Fiona Mcleod, *The Divine Adventure: Iona*, Duffield, New York, 1910.

7 Hospitality
1 The *Sayings of the Fathers* translated from the Greek by Pelagius, and John 13.
2 Translated by Diarmuid O'Laoghaire in a collection of Irish graces published by Mount Melleray Monastery, Ireland.
3 Adamnan, *Life of Saint Columba*, Llanerch, 1988.

8 Real Men, Women and Families
1 In *Pastoral Care Ministries Newsletter*. USA, 1994.
2 See Miranda Green, *Symbol and Image in Celtic Religious Art*, Routledge, 1992, chapter 2: 'The Female Image'; and chapter 4: 'The Male Image'.
3 This theme is explored by William Anderson, in *The Green Man*, HarperCollins, 1990.
4 Now at St Hilaire-le-Grand.
5 John Scotus Eriugena, *The Division of Nature*, ed. and trans. I. P. Sheldon, Williams, Paris, 1987.
6 In Tomas O'Fiaich, *Columbanus in His Own Words*, Veritas, 1974, p. 112.

7 Report by Colin Moreton in *The Church Times*, 19 August 1994.
8 This theme is explored further in Noragh Jones, *Power of Raven, Wisdom of Serpent: Celtic Women's Spirituality*, Floris Books, 1994.
9 In Whitley Stokes' *Lives of the Saints from the Book of Lismore*, Anecdota Onodiensa, Medieval and Modern Series, Part V, OUP, New York, 1890.
10 See Carl Jung, *Modern Man in Search of a Soul*, p. 19.
11 Adamnan, *Life of Saint Columba*, Llanerch, 1988.
12 Alexander Carmichael, *Carmina Gadelica*, Floris Books, 1992. Notes on Prayer 77.

9 A Cherished Creation
1 1 Corinthians 7:8.
2 Claus Westermann, *Creation*, SCM, 1974, p. 52.
3 L. White Jr, 'The Historical Roots of our Ecological Crisis', Appendix A, in Francis Schaeffer and Udo Middelmann, *Pollution and the Death of Man*, Crossway, 1992.
4 Andrew Walker, *Creation and the Cross*, Rural Theology Association Report, 1991.
5 Esther de Waal, *A World Made Whole*, Fount, 1991.
6 H. J. Massingham, *The Tree of Life*, Chapman and Hall, 1943.
7 Quoted in Christopher Bamford and William Parker Marsh, *Celtic Christianity: Ecology and Holiness*, Floris Books, 1986.
8 English translation in Patrick Thomas, *Candle in the Darkness*, Gomer, 1993.
9 Alexander Carmichael, *Carmina Gadelica*, Floris Books, 1992; note on Prayer No. 222.
10 Donald Evans, quoted in Thomas, op. cit.
11 Heathcote Williams, *Falling for a Dolphin*, Jonathan Cape, 1991.
12 Quoted in Robert Van de Weyer, *Celtic Fire*, DLT, 1990.
13 John Scotus Eriugena, *The Voice of the Eagle*, Floris Books, 1990, ed. Christopher Bamford.
14 Carmichael, op. cit.
15 Ron Ferguson, *Chasing the Wild Goose*, Fount, 1989.
16 See Jürgen Moltmann, *The Future of Creation*, SCM Press, 1979.
17 See W. Heisenberg, *The Physicist's Conception of Nature*, quoted in Moltmann, op. cit., p. 128.
18 Adamnan, *Life of Saint Columba*, Llanerch, 1988.
19 Community of Aidan and Hilda, *Way of Life*, 1994.
20 Community of Aidan and Hilda, 1994.
21 *Healing the Earth*, Community of Aidan and Hilda, 1994.

10 The Cross in Creation
1 Lev Gillett.
2 Andrew Walker, in *Towards a Theology of Creation*, Rural Theology Association, 1993. Quoting M. Fox, *Original Blessing*, Bear & Co., New Mexico, 1983.
3 Robin Flower, *The Irish Tradition*, Clarendon, 1947.

4 Quoted in A. M. Allchin and Esther De Waal, *Threshold of Light*, DLT, 1991.
5 'The Dream of the Rood', in *Brother Caedmon*, Sylvia Mundahl-Harris, 1982.
6 'The Crucifixion', in *Ancient Irish Poetry*, Kuno Meyer (trans.), Constable, 1994.
7 Allchin and De Waal, op. cit.

11 A World of Sacrament
1 *The Christian Democrat*, June 1994.
2 Selwyn Hughes, *Every Day With Jesus*, 19 November 1994, Crusade for World Revival.
3 Ron Ferguson, *Chasing the Wild Goose*, Fount, 1989.
4 David Adam, *Borderlands*, SPCK, 1994.
5 George MacDonald, *A Dish of Orts*, George Newnes, London, 1905. Quoted in Noel Dermot O'Donoghue, *The Mountain Behind the Mountain*, T & T Clark, 1993.
6 O'Donoghue, op. cit.
7 Brother Aidan, in *Catholic World Report*, March 1993.
8 O'Donoghue, op. cit.
9 H. Carpenter (ed.), *The Letters of J. R. R. Tolkien*, London, 1981, no. 81.
10 C. S. Lewis, in *Pilgrim's Regress*, Geoffrey Bles, 1944, pp. 152–3.
11 Leonie Caldecott, in *Catholic World Report*, 1993.
12 A Celtic poem in *A Celtic Miscellany*, Kenneth Hewlestone Jackson, (ed.), Penguin, 1971.
13 Leanne Payne, *Real Presence: The Holy Spirit in the Works of C. S. Lewis*, Monarch, 1988.
14 *Carmina Gadelica*, quoted in O'Donoghue, op. cit., p. 16.
15 Alexander Carmichael, *Carmina Gadelica*, Floris Books, 1992.

12 The Eternal Struggle
1 Bede, 'Life of Cuthbert', in *The Age of Bede*, Penguin Classics, 1983.
2 Ibid.
3 Ibid.
4 Adamnan, *Life of Saint Columba*, Llanerch, 1988.
5 Lesslie Newbigin, *The Gospel in a Pluralist Society*, SPCK, 1990.
6 This is explored in Richard Rohr and Joseph Martos, *The Wild Man's Journey*, St Anthony Press, USA, 1992.
7 Ludwig Bieler (ed.), *The Irish Penitentials*, Dublin, 1963.
8 Gerard Murphy, *Early Irish Lyrics*, Oxford, 1956, pp. 54–7.
9 Lucy Menzies, *Saint Columba of Iona*, Llanerch, 1992.

13 The Encircling Three
1 Irenaeus of Lyons, *The Demonstration of the Apostolic Preaching 6*, quoted in Olivier Clemont, *The Roots of Christian Mysticism*, New City, 1993.

2 Mrs Alexander's hymn version of 'St Patrick's Breastplate'.
3 Sammy Horner, *Celtic Praise album T-Allt Ruadh*, Daybreak Music Ltd, 1994.
4 Alexander Carmichael, *Carmina Gadelica*, Floris Books, 1992.
5 *Worship for Mondays and Trinity Season*, Community of Aidan and Hilda, 1994.

14 The Wild Goose
1 John L. Bell and Graham A. Maule, *Heaven Shall Not Wait*, Wild Goose Publications, 1987.
2 Thomas Taylor (ed.), *The Life of Samson of Dol*, Llanerch, 1991.
3 *The Confession of St Patrick*, Floris Books, 1993.
4 Adamnan, *Life of Saint Columba*, Llanerch, 1988, Book 3, chapter 19.

15 Signs and Wonders
1 *The Miracles of Bishop Ninia*, in John MacQueen, *St Nynia*, Polygon, 1990.
2 Adamnan, *Life of Saint Columba*, Llanerch, 1988.
3 *Confessions of St Patrick*, in Noel O'Donoghue, *Aristocracy of Soul*, DLT, 1987.
4 *The Voyage of St Brendan*, Floris Books, 1991.
5 Bede, *Ecclesiastical History of the English People*, Penguin, 1989.
6 *Confessions of St Patrick*, op.cit.

16 The Prophetic Spirit
1 Adamnan, *Life of Saint Columba*, Llanerch, 1988.
2 *A Directory of the Religious Life in the Church of England*. Advisory Council on Relations of Bishops and Religious Communities, 1990.
3 Renewal of baptismal vows, Weston Priory, New England, USA.
4 Joan M. Kendall.

17 Healing
1 Adamnan, *Life of Saint Columba*, Llanerch, 1988.
2 Bede, 'Life of St Cuthbert', in *The Age of Bede*, Penguin Classics, 1983.
3 Ibid.
4 Alexander Carmichael, *Carmina Gadelica*, Floris Books, 1992, Prayers Nos 433 and 429.

18 A Church without Walls
1 'The Confessions of St Patrick', in Alannah Hopkin, *The Living Legend of St Patrick*, Grafton, 1989.
2 Lucy Menzies, *Columba*, Llanerch, 1989.
3 Anne Warinhamp, *Hilda: an Anglo Saxon Chronicle*, Marshall, Morgan & Seott, 1989.
4 David Gwenalt Jones.

5 F. E. Warren, *The Liturgy and Ritual of the Celtic Church*, Boydell, 1987, p. 33.
6 Revelation 2 and 3.
7 Warren, op. cit., p. 85.

19 Compassion for the Poor
1 Unattributed, in Robert Van der Weyer, *Celtic Fire*, DLT, 1990.
2 Cogitosus, *Life of St Brigid the Virgin*, in Liam De Paov (trans.), *Saint Patrick's World*, Four Courts Press, 1993.
3 Gerlad, *Description of Wales*, cited, I think, in Wade-Evans (ed.), *Life of St David*, SPCK, 1923.
4 Alexander Carmichael, *Carmina Gadelica*, Floris Books, 1992, notes on Prayer 77.

20 Vocations for All
1 James P. Mackey, *Introduction to Celtic Spirituality*, T & T Clark, 1989.
2 A. B. Scott, *The Pictish Nation: Its People and Its Church*, Foulis, 1918.
3 Bede, *Ecclesiastical History of the English People*, Oxford, 1969.
4 A. M. Allchin *et al.*, *Solitude and Communion*, Fairacres, 1975.

21 One Church
1 F. E. Warren, *The Liturgy and Ritual of the Celtic Church*, Boydell, 1987, p. 94.
2 Joceline, 'The Life of Kentigern' in *Two Celtic Saints*, Llanerch, 1989, p. 54.
3 Matthew 5–7.
4 Swete, *The Church and Its Ministry*, p. 107.
5 'Catalogue of the Saints of Ireland', in J. F. Kenney, *Sources for the Early History of Ireland*, vol. 1, New York, 1968.
6 Magnus Magnusson, *Lindisfarne the Cradle Island*, Oriel Press, 1985.
7 Twelfth-century Irish in *A Celtic Miscellany*, Penguin, 1991.
8 'Catalogue of the Saints of Ireland', op.cit.
9 G. S. M. Walker (ed.), *Sancti Columbani Opera*, Institute for Advanced Studies, Dublin, 1957 contains the Latin text of all surviving works of Columbanus.

22 'Go-with-the-flow' Evangelism
1 *Decade News*: News of the Decade of Evangelism from the Church of England General Synod's Board of Mission, January 1994.
2 Ian Bradley, *The Celtic Way*, DLT, 1993.
3 Thomas Taylor (ed.), *The Life of Samson of Dol*, Llanerch, 1991.
4 Patrick *Confessions*, in Liam de Paov, *Saint Patrick's World*, Four Courts Press, 1993.
5 Adamnan, *Life of Saint Columba*, Llanerch, 1988, Book 3, chapter 15.

6 Bede, *Ecclesiastical History of the English People*, Oxford, 1969.
7 *Church Times*, December 1992.
8 Arthur Wright, *St Aidan*. This old life of St Aidan, written in verse, is long out of print. It is quoted in *Daily Readings* on St Aidan, published by the Northumbria Community.
9 Ray Simpson, *The Mantle of St Aidan*.
10 Hugh Montefiore, *The Gospel and Contemporary Culture* (Introduction), Mowbray, 1992.

23 Healing of the Nations
1 Gwynfor Evans.
2 Alice Stopford Green.
3 Joan Tapsfield, *An English Pilgrim in Northern Ireland 1977–1992*, Grosvenor Books, 1993.
4 In Lucy Menzies, *Columba*, Llanerch, 1989.
5 Vida D. Scudder, Introduction to *Bede's Ecclesiastical History of the English Nation*, Everyman, 1930.
6 Stephen Lawhead, *Arthur* (an historical novel), Lion, 1989.
7 See, for example, Douglas Johnston, *Religion, the Missing Dimension of Statecraft*, 1994, available from Grosvenor Books.

24 Angels
1 David Adam, *Borderlands*, SPCK, 1994.
2 Hope Macdonald, *When Angels Appear*, Marshalls, 1984.
3 *Daily Mail*, 13 February 1995.
4 Leslie Hardinge, *The Celtic Church in Britain*, SPCK, 1973, p. 78.
5 Bede, 'Life of Cuthbert', in *The Age of Bede*, Penguin Classics, 1985.
6 Alexander Carmichael, *Carmina Gadelica*, Floris Books, 1992, Prayer No. 77.
7 Carmichael's notes on the above.
8 Community of Aidan and Hilda, *Worship for Michaelmas*.

25 Triumphant Dying
1 Bede, *Ecclesiastical History of the English People*, Penguin, 1989.
2 Adamnan, *Life of Saint Columba*, Llanerch, 1988.
3 Bede, 'The Life and Miracles of Cuthbert', in *The Age of Bede*, Penguin Classics, 1985.
4 Bede, *Ecclesiastical History*, op. cit.
5 Iain Macdonald (ed.), *Brendan*, Floris Books, 1991.
6 *Preparing a Good Death*, Community of Aidan and Hilda, 1994.
7 Alexander Carmichael, *Carmina Gadelica*, Floris Books, 1992.
8 *Hebridean Altars*.
9 *Traditional Irish Prayers*, Mount Melleray Monastery.
10 Donald Swann.

Further Reading

Adamnan, *Life of Saint Columba*, Llanerch, 1988.
David Adam, *Borderlands*, SPCK, 1991.
Ailred and Jocelyn, *The Lives of St Ninian and St Kentigern*, Llanerch, 1989.
Ian Bradley, *The Celtic Way*, DLT, 1993.
John Marsden (trans.), *The Illustrated Bede*, Macmillan, 1989.
Michael Mitton, *Restoring the Woven Chord*, DLT, 1995.
Liam de Paov, *Saint Patrick's World*, Four Courts Press, 1993.
Edward C. Sellner, *Wisdom of the Celtic Saints*, Ave Maria Press, 1993.
Thomas Taylor (ed.), *The Life of Samson of Dol*, Llanerch, 1991.
Shirley Toulson, *The Celtic Year*, Element, 1993.
Esther de Waal, *A World Made Whole*, Fount, 1991.
Robert Van der Weyer, *Celtic Fire*, DLT, 1990.